# the comfort zone juliet bawden

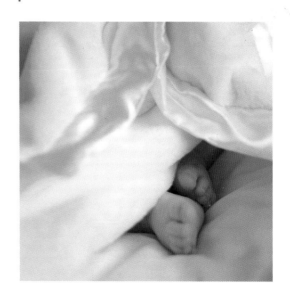

# the comfort zone juliet bawden

## over 30 quick and easy textile projects for the home

Photography by Jon Bouchier

COLLINS & BROWN

*For Lily Gooch, who encompasses style and glamour with comfort.*

First published in Great Britain in 2001
by Collins & Brown Limited
London House
Great Eastern Wharf
Parkgate Road
London SW11 4NQ

1 3 5 7 9 8 6 4 2

British Library Cataloguing-in-Publication Data:
A catalogue record for this book is available from the British Library.

ISBN 1 85585 893 2

Conceived, edited and designed by Collins & Brown Limited

Editor: Gillian Haslam
Copy Editor: Lisa Dyer
Proof Reader: Alison Wormleighton
Designer: Christine Wood
Photographer: Jon Bouchier (photographs on pages 7, 24, 25, 59,
66, 67 and 69 centre and right by Marie-Louise Avery)
Stylist: Dirk Fuhrmann
Artwork: Anthony Duke

Reproduction by Classic Scan Pte Ltd, Singapore
Printed and bound in China by L-Rex Printing Company
This book was typeset using Futura and Bembo

# Acknowledgments

This book has been a real pleasure to create. Lots of people have been involved – those who made the projects and those who helped to create the book.

On the days when we shot the photographs we had a great deal of fun, although the catchphrase of the book has to be 'I think it needs another iron' and we have all put on weight because Dirk our stylist makes the best cakes I have ever tasted. They are true comfort food.

Thank you to Jon Bouchier who has produced such sumptuous photographs, Christine Wood for designing the book so beautifully and for art directing and to Gillian Haslam for keeping the whole project going and for unfailing good humour. A big thank you to Dirk Fuhrmann (who, being the youngest, got teased the most) for all his time and sensitivity in helping to produce exquisite pictures. Thanks to Lisa Dyer who had the worst job sorting the manuscript at the end.

I would also like to thank Jane Will, who not only loaned her beautiful house but 'discovered' Dirk. I cannot thank Shirley White enough, who coaxed and cuddled her daughter Georgina into modelling perfectly – also a big thank you to Georgina.

Thanks also go to:
Beryl Miller, who must be the best seamstress in the UK,
Josephine Ryan, for the loan of her lovely house,
Andrea Bailey, for the felt slippers,
Jean Fellows, for the cross-stitch projects,
Alice Wilson, for all her dyeing and felting,
Jessica Moxley, for knitting the bathroom rug and beading the laundry bag.

# Contents

# Introduction

This is a book about creating stylish comfort in the home. If we are not comfortable, we are not happy, and yet so often people live in a style that is sold to them by the latest magazine or television programme. To create comfort, one needs to let the senses become unfettered by modern living – the pollution in the cities, the unnatural smells of disinfectant, air fresheners and deodorants in our offices and homes, the synthetic materials that clothe our bodies. We have become frightened by one of our most potent senses, that of smell. We allow our houses to be full of junk and clutter that we do not need and do not really want. We use man-made fibres, which produce static and feel unpleasant to the touch. In this book we have attempted to redress the balance by offering ways for you to create a home full of comfort and sensuality through the use of colour, texture, pattern and scent.

I trained as a textile designer and my great passion in life is textiles. By using fabrics simply but creatively you can change your home environment for the better; as a result many of the projects in this book are based on sewing or needlework of some kind, and they all revolve round the main living areas of a home. Some of the projects are very simple – it is just the idea behind the creation that counts – whereas others are a little more complex, but all will add comfort to your home and the way in which you live.

*Felted slippers on a bed of soft mohair throws create an immediate feeling of comfort. Felt is a traditional material often used to make hats and slippers, while mohair is valued for its warmth and lightness.*

the essence
of comfort

# The Essence of Comfort

Home comfort is created by the environment which surrounds us – light, colour, texture, pattern and scent all have a part to play. This chapter explains how these different elements work together to create a welcoming and comfortable home, and how to make the most of them.

Colour is one of the first things we notice when we enter a room. It can be introduced through the paint on the walls, the soft furnishings and the floor coverings. The following pages explain how to use subdued and muted colours to create a relaxing look, and how to layer the colours, from the darkest shade to the lightest hue.

Texture is all-important in our choice of soft furnishings. Here we explore the wide range of fabrics now available, from cotton – either crisp and new or soft and gently aged – to tactile suede,

*Flowers do not have to be complicated or formal. Some of the most pleasing arrangements are made using roses and lavender sprigs cut from the garden. Choose simple jugs or vases in complementary colours and elegant shapes.*

from plush velvet to comfy fleece. From simple felt to luxurious chenille, there is a fabric to suit every room and every mood. Pattern works closely with colour and texture. Subtle pattern can be introduced through a faint sheen on a fabric, by mixing printed fabrics in the same colours or through the use of knitted textures.

The light in a home can be softly filtered through translucent voiles and muslins, hung in sheer layers at a window, or controlled by carefully selecting lamps and shades to provide just the right degree of brightness. Candles, too, have an important role in creating atmosphere, from small buckets or vases filled with elegant tapers to thick church candles or bowls of floating candles.

*For a fine, flickering light, place candle tapers in sand in a glass vase. Take care that when the tapers burn down, they do not touch the glass.*

Scent provides the perfect finishing touch for any comfort zone. Candles, flowers, potpourris, incense sticks, soaps and bath oils are just some of the ways to introduce relaxing or sensuous aromas to the home.

*Aromatic bath oils combine a feeling of luxury with soothing aromas. Pour oils into pretty glass jars and display on a window ledge so sunlight can shine through and enhance their colours.*

Finally, when creating a 'comfort zone', take time to enjoy it. By all means invest in luxury by doing the little things that mean a lot, like ironing and starching sheets, buying flowers, lighting candles and playing restful music. But most importantly, take time to truly relax and tune out from the stresses of the day. The home you create should be a haven from the turmoil of the world and enable you to recharge your energy levels and gain a little peace of mind.

# Colour

Colour and the way it affects our lives is of prime importance in the pursuit of comfort. Some colours work together, while others jar, making a discordant environment. Colour affects our emotional well-being and can help create an atmosphere of relaxation or of tension. The projects and interiors shown throughout this book use a very particular colour scheme of soft shades of pinks, blues, lavenders, greys and creams, which create a feeling of warmth and comfort in the cold months of the year and coolness and freshness for the hotter times.

Research shows that people have particular responses to different colours, which has led manufacturers and advertisers to favour certain ones. Fashion plays a part in colour preferences, too, and a huge industry is devoted to forecasting what colour fabrics we will use to decorate our homes and cover our bodies. The forecasters also influence what paint colours will be made.

Most interior decorators use different terms to identify groups of colours, and the terms listed here may prove instrumental in devising your own colour scheme.

*Complementary colours* are contrasting colours that are opposite each other on the colour wheel. Examples are red and green, blue and orange, and yellow and violet. Complementary colours usually make a powerful statement.

*Harmonious colours* are those that are close to one another in the spectrum, such as greens, turquoises and blues. These colours work well together and make a pleasing colour scheme. Harmonious colours are used throughout this book to create a calm, comfortable visual effect.

*Neutral colours* are technically only black, white and grey, but in interior design they also include browns, beiges, creams and off-white.

*Accent colours* are used to emphasize a colour scheme. Usually in a shade that contrasts with the main interior colour, the accent colour is used in small but potent amounts.

*Colour value* is often linked to the tone of a colour – that is, whether it is dark or light. The tone can be changed by adding black or white to a colour. When two pigments of equal intensity are mixed together, the resulting colour is darker.

## Colour Symbolism

You may like to consider decorating your home in colours that will echo the function of a room. For example, blue, a popular, restful colour, is often chosen for bathrooms and bedrooms.

*Red* is the symbol of fire, passion, rage, danger and destruction. The Romans used a red flag in battle to stimulate the endocrine glands, which in turn released adrenaline and helped to increase the energy level. Red is an active, dramatic and stimulating colour.

*Yellow* is associated with the intellect – it is the colour of perception rather than reason. To Hindus, the yellow-orange robes worn by monks symbolize serenity and renunciation. A murky yellow, however, is associated with sickness, treason and deception, as well as cowardice.

*Green* is the colour of hope, new life, energy, fertility, growth. It is a restful colour, and often used on hospital walls. The term 'greenhorn' means a person who is inexperienced and new to something. Dark green signifies envy and superstition. Soft greens, such as sage and moss, are good neutral background colours for carpets and sofas. They give a feeling of being grounded and in touch with nature.

*Blue* is the colour of intuition. It symbolizes true devotion, sincerity and calmness. The passivity associated with blue may also be the reason it is considered the colour of sadness, as in 'feeling blue'.

*Purple* is the colour of majesty, dignity and royalty, but it is also the colour of rage.

## Restful Schemes

Subdued colours or neutral schemes create a calm framework in which to live one's life. the most harmonious schemes use the same or similar ('harmonious') colours in different tones, or they use different colours of the same tonal value. The amount of any one colour used will affect the other colours and consequently the overall look. When choosing furnishing fabrics, for example, place fabric samples next to each other, one at a time, noticing the changes in tone. Experiment with a combination of colours and differing quantities of each colour until you are happy with the result.

Most of the projects in this book complement one another easily and can coexist without visual conflict. A neutral background will also allow you to inject a touch of strong colour, as there will be no colour to compete with it.

## Choosing Wall Colour

Each interior designer has his or her own unique approach to using colour, so be confident and follow your own instincts and preferences. The easiest way to discover your likes and dislikes is to look at paint charts and select a range, or palette, that you like. Buy sample pots of the colours and paint them on the walls. Go into the room at different times of day, and in different lights, to see which colours you prefer.

A good idea is to choose a paint range which has several similar tones of one colour. This way you can use the lightest tone on the ceiling, the next on the walls and the third on the picture rail and coving. On walls, neutral colours that are comfortable to live with include cream, linen, stone and off-white. White can be too strong and bright, especially in the cold light of Northern European countries.

*A swathe of silky fabrics with one colour flowing subtly into the next.*

*For comfort, choose colours which happily sit next to one another,*

*rather than eye-jarring contrasts.*

# Texture

With a limited colour palette, it is essential to make the most of texture. The more simple the fabric and colour choices, the more important its role. The clever mixing of textures will make an interior scheme look and feel more interesting. Materials that are the same colour but which have their own unique texture will reflect light in different ways. A dress silk, for example, will look shiny and smooth, whereas a silk dupion, which has a slub in its weave, will look more matt and uneven. However, texture is more than just visual – it is about the touch and sensuality of materials. A fabulous smooth suede or a cosy matted felt feels very different from a floaty voile or a heavyweight linen; a cotton lawn pillowcase will contrast with the fluffiness of angora or the softness of cashmere. Thus the layering of various textures not only adds to the excitement of an interior but creates a 'comfort zone' at the same time.

Fabrics that would have been considered utilitarian in the past, such as hessian (burlap) or loosely woven linen, are now thought of as highly desirable and used by interior decorators all over the world. This move is partly to do with changing times – interiors are less cluttered than ever before, and most people want to avoid the chintzes and flounces so closely associated with earlier eras. We want simplicity and comfort, nothing too distracting and jarring to the senses. Although man-made fibres are improving all the time, such as with luxurious fake furs, it is the natural textures of wool, cotton and wood which breathe life into our homes, and which we, as human beings, ultimately feel most at home with.

# Pattern

Pattern surrounds us in everyday life. A wealth of shapes and designs appear in nature, including leaves, fruits and flowers, which have long been an inspiration to artists and designers. These images, stylized and adapted, can be found in such materials as textiles, wallpaper, murals and tiles. Although many interior schemes use printed patterns, pattern does not need to be so obvious. The patterns in this book are mainly self-coloured ones that are woven into the fabric itself, such as damask, or that use an embroidered or appliquéd repeated design worked in a harmonizing colour to the background. Soft muted patterns can also be achieved by using faded fabrics or hand-dyeing materials. Contrasting edges, such as bound borders or chenille trims, create an understated, subtle pattern. There is an element of nostalgia and warmth in creating a new pattern from recycled clothing or antique lace.

Repeating a theme throughout an interior is one way of using pattern. Keep to the same type of fabric or the same pattern in harmonious colours to prevent the look from becoming overbearing. For example, a 'quiet' way to repeat a pattern is by using a mixture of ornate and delicate lace to decorate cushions and pillowcases in the same room. Look at a printed or patterned fabric and consider using the wrong side if the pattern looks softer or more in keeping with the look you wish to achieve. Faded and antique fabrics often have a more distressed or aged pattern that has a charm of its own and works well in neutral interiors.

Do not be afraid to mix patterns or prints of different scale – if the pieces look good side by side, then they will work with each other. If you are at all unsure, choose patterns that have the same or similar background colours. Place pieces of fabric next to each another, removing some and replacing them with others, until you find a combination that works well.

*As this selection of fabrics demonstrates, texture and pattern can change the character of*

*a fabric. Although all in a similar colour range, the appearance of these fabrics is affected*

*by the surface pattern and texture and the way in which light plays upon them.*

# Lighting

When thinking about lighting an environment, consider 'fitness for purpose' – rooms where you work, wash or cook need to be brighter than rooms where you sleep, relax or dine. Use natural light as much as possible. When buying a house, look at the size of the windows. Do they let in sufficient light? Try to keep windows free from heavy drapes in summer. A judicious placing of voile curtains and louvred blinds allows natural light to filter gently into a room. Glass, too, affects the way in which light enters a room. Stained glass will produce striking colours and patterns on a wall. Sandblasted glass gives a pretty diffused effect, especially when used on internal doors, where it also offers a modicum of privacy.

Candles are ideal for creating ambience and soft lighting. In the bathroom, surround the bath with scented candles for a deeply relaxing experience. On a dining table, arrange candle tapers in a container of sand to create a pretty twinkly effect, or place large church candles in storm lanterns to create an extra glow. Floating candles in a bowl of water create a lovely focal point on a table, especially if you use a glass bowl so that the flickering flames reflect in the water.

Used skilfully, artificial lighting can also make a room more comfortable. Table lamps, in particular, can be positioned to cast light onto soft furnishings, enhancing the mood and adding warmth to the room. As with colour, there are some terms useful to know when considering which light sources to use.

*Ambient light* surrounds us and does not come from any obvious source. It does not usually create shadow. Ambient light sources should always be as discreet as possible.

*Accent lighting* highlights a room's features, and is often used above a painting or to show off a display or collection. It is directional and thus restricted to a single area, working within a room that already has ambient lighting.

*Task lighting* is the lighting we use when performing activities, such as writing, sewing and cooking, where we need increased visibility. Good task lighting will prevent eye strain and help you focus on the job in hand. The source of task lighting should be hidden, as its glare will distract the eyes. Task lighting should be fitted with an opaque shade or shield of some kind. In kitchens it is often hidden beneath the upper cupboard units.

*Decorative lighting* has little to do with creating comfort in the home, but aesthetic beauty has its own rewards. This type of lighting can be as extravagant as a chandelier or as entertaining as a neon light sculpture or lava lamp.

*Kinetic lighting* is light that moves and flickers, such as the flames of a fire or that of a candle. The proliferation of candle shops over the last decade has very much to do with the desire to create a softly lit, relaxing space in today's high-stress world.

*Sunlight filters through shutters to make beautiful shadows. The way in which light is filtered creates different moods in a room – translucent fabric at a window softens shadows whereas shutters make a more regular pattern.*

*Floating candles create romantic, soft lighting, especially when combined with water and individual rose petals. A wide, shallow bowl provides the best effect.*

# Scent

Even more so than colour or texture, scent strikes a unique primitive chord in each one of us. No one has exactly the same associations with smells as another. The people we love smell good to us, babies are born with the ability to recognize their mother's unique smell and sexual attraction is bound up in smell. It is important to remember that natural smells are useful, necessary and pleasurable, especially in a world where we deodorize and sanitize away virtually every odour from our homes and bodies. Scents quicken our senses and act as stimuli, and this is why the old trick of making fresh coffee or baking bread when you are showing potential buyers around a house is so successful. And, as Victor Hugo said, 'Nothing awakens a reminiscence like an odour'.

Get back in touch with the smells you love best. For me, it is the smell of fir trees and damp hedgerows, which take me back to hiding under the bushes in my grandparents' garden. For others it may be the smell of freshly cut grass, which is such a popular scent that some manufacturers have bottled it as a room fragrance. But why buy scent in a bottle when you can have the real thing?

*A fragrant winter potpourri is made from small dried oranges, orange peel, fir cones and cooking aromatics such as cinnamon sticks and cloves.*

*Fresh rose petals and sprigs of lavender make a pleasing summer potpourri. When making potpourri, choose a bowl suitable for the season – here a soapstone bowl complements the soft shades of summer, while a black ceramic platter enhances the deep colours of winter.*

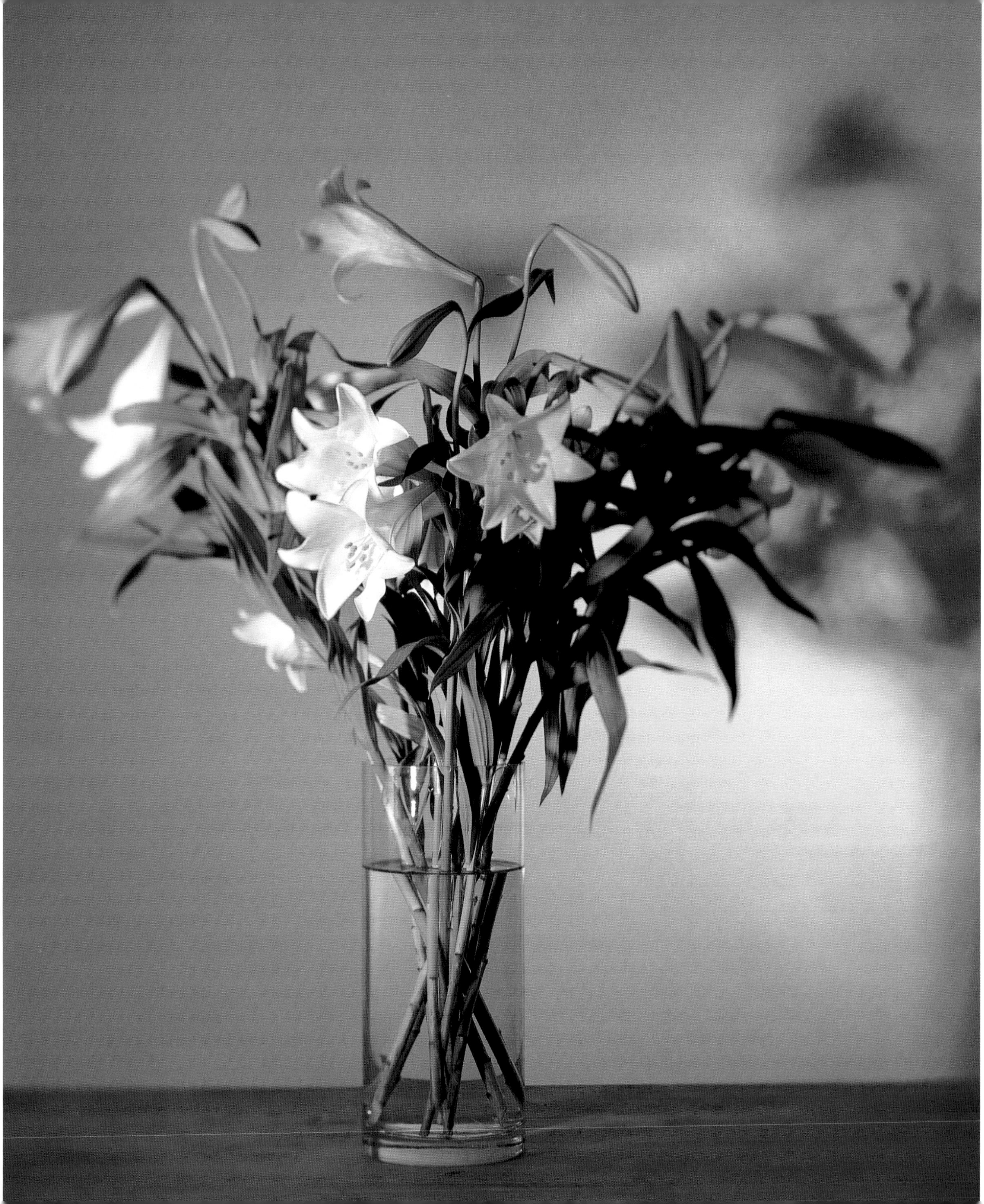

Create sensuality and comfort in the home by adding fresh rose petals to a bowl of floating candles or by tying sprigs of lavender together and hanging them in the wardrobe or bathroom. Or make herbal sachets and place them in drawers to freshen clothes. Buy the best soap you can afford as it is a relatively inexpensive everyday luxury.

Try to develop your sense of smell. Take time to enjoy walks in the rain or at the beginning of each season. Autumn, in particular, has a slightly musty earth smell of its own. Make an effort to get outdoors, especially in the country or by the sea, but if that is not practical, create a haven for the senses indoors. Grow fresh herbs on the windowsill or fill a room with scented blooms – lilies and home-grown roses are particularly appealing. Create a summer potpourri using rosebuds and petals or a winter version using dried orange peel, cinnamon sticks and fir cones.

As well as working to put good smells into your home, be sure to dispel bad ones. Stale kitchen odours can permeate an entire apartment or house so make sure your home is well ventilated. Sometimes there is nothing as refreshing and invigorating as a breeze blowing the scent of spring through an open window.

*Lilies are not only supremely elegant in appearance, but also possess the most heavenly aroma. For pure simplicity, display them in a tall, plain glass tank. When buying fresh flowers, always choose ones which have not been forced – they will have a far better scent and will last longer.*

*Beautiful soap is one of those small, everyday luxuries that most of us can afford. What could be better than the feeling of good soap against the skin? To please the eye, display the soaps in a toning hand-crafted ceramic bowl in the bathroom.*

bedrooms

# The bedroom *is your most private and personal space. It is the room you escape to when you are tired, ill or upset or just in need of a catnap. It is the first space you see when you wake up in the morning, and the last you see at night. As we spend one-third of our lives in bed, this room should be perfect.*

*Calm colours on the walls, a good mattress (and this does not mean a soft one) on which to sink after a hard day's work, and warm woolly blankets in winter or cool cotton sheets in summer are necessary for a comfortable bedroom. Natural fabrics allow the skin to 'breathe'. Use 100 per cent cotton or linen bedlinen, as it is so much more pleasant to the touch than poly-cotton mixes. Invest in a good duvet cover and pillows – there is nothing more likely to ruin a night's sleep than lumpy or hard pillows. Buy at least one large square pillow per person.*

*The cream and linen-coloured wallpaper is echoed by the cream coloured cashmere/woollen blanket and the white bedlinen. The striped and piqué pillowcases add interest to the monotones of the bedlinen.*

These Shaker-style pillows are made from the finest cotton. The traditional cross-stitch design is usually worked in bright red or royal blue, but here the pale fawn-coloured thread adds interest with a subtlety not usually present in cross-stitch.

These are wonderful for leaning against when reading in bed, and they look very stylish as well. Ensure that your bedside lamp is at the correct height for night-time reading.

Make the room a haven. Avoid clutter by having plenty of storage for clothes and shoes and keep all personal items out of sight. Use rugs or a fitted carpet to make the room as soundproof as possible and try to sleep far away from busy roads (the back of a house is usually quieter than the front). Because bedrooms are usually upstairs or away from shared family rooms, they can be decorated to suit the personality and style of those who occupy them. In this chapter projects have been selected that add a little style and personalize a space without sacrificing comfort. There are snow-white pillowcases, some embroidered in ecru, others decorated using vintage lace, as well as wonderful throws and blankets, and we have not forgotten babies, who need comfort too.

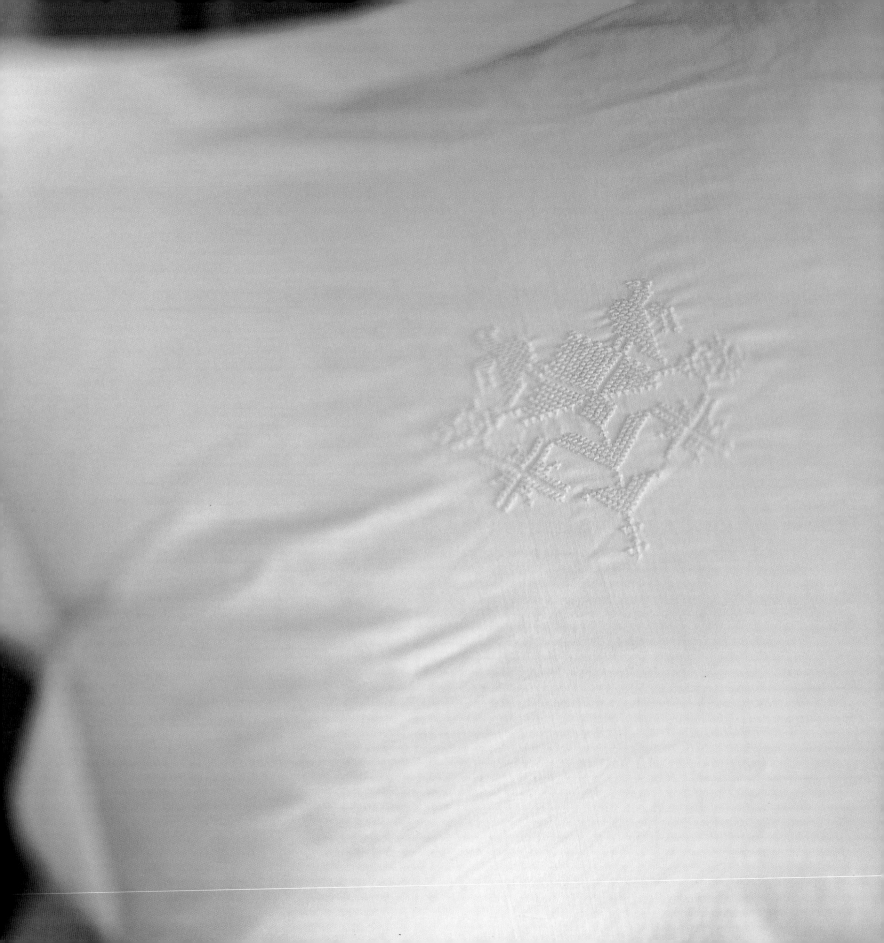

# Cross-stitch Pillowcase

Square pillows are the height of comfort – large enough to rest one's upper body and head on or to sink into at the end of a long hard day. Cross-stitch, one of the simplest ways of achieving complex designs, creates an elegant effect, and cream-on-white is always a winning combination for tranquil sleep. The traditional bird-and-flower motif shown here is classically simple and quick to stitch. After completing one pillowcase, why not embroider other white ones in the same cream thread. The cross-stitch designs may differ, but they will look pretty together if the same colour combination is used.

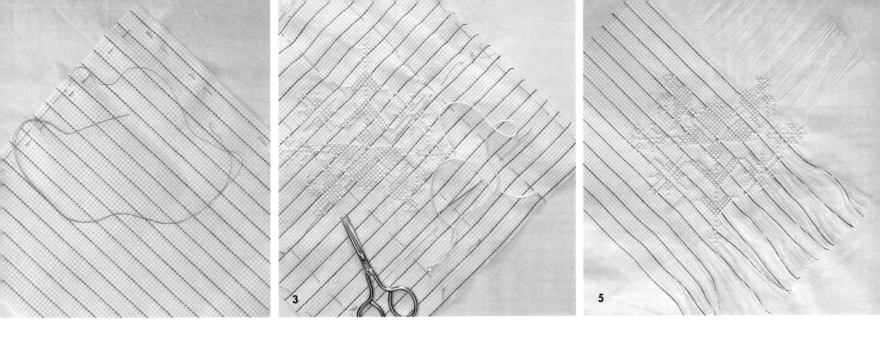

**one**  First find the exact centre of the pillowcase. Measure the pillowcase diagonally from the top right corner to the bottom left corner, marking the centre. Repeat across the opposite corners. The marks should coincide at the dead centre of the pillowcase. Another easy way to find the centre is to press the pillowcase along each diagonal, marking the point where they intersect with a pin. Alternatively, if you think it may be uncomfortable to sleep with your face directly on the embroidery, stitch a cross-stitch border design around the edges of the pillowcase.

**two**  Pin the fine waste canvas as a diamond in the centre of the pillowcase. Use a running stitch to baste the waste canvas in place, making sure you stitch through one layer of fabric only. If desired, stretch the piece in an embroidery hoop.

**three**  Using the waste canvas as a guide for the stitch positions, and using three strands of embroidery thread (floss), follow the cross-stitch chart given (see left) to embroider the design. Each square in the chart represents one stitch. To start a stitch, pull the needle through from the front of the fabric, leaving an end of about 5 cm (2 in) on the right side. Hold this end securely while working the first stitch. When several stitches have been completed, the end can be threaded onto a needle and pushed through to the back of the cloth and woven through the worked stitches.

**four**  Cross-stitch is generally accomplished either by working along a row in one direction with half stitches and then coming back in the other direction, or by making rows of complete stitches. The tops of the stitches should always slant in the same direction to prevent the work from looking untidy. Work from the centre outwards to give a more even look to the finished work. Where possible, bring the needle up through unworked fabric and down through holes where stitches have already been worked.

**five**  When the design is complete, carefully pull out the waste canvas threads and press the pillowcase.

**L a c e   P i l l o w c a s e s**   Old lace is still one of those commodities that are not hard to come by, as textiles are often considered less valuable than other antiques. Look for antique lace scraps and trims in thrift shops, markets, house auctions and rummage sales. Often a garment may be full of holes or unwearable but the lace can be reclaimed. Look for heavyweight curtain and furnishing lace, taken from old runners, antimacassars and the like, as well as more delicate or intricate lace from clothing.

Heirloom laces, such as those inherited from a grandmother or cut from your child's christening gown, can be used in a commemorative pillow. The narrow cream lace trim used here was brought back from Belgium during the First World War by my great-uncle as a gift for my great-aunt. The lace on the bolster was cut from a very moth-eaten Victorian petticoat. The wide heavyweight lace trim used for some of the pillows pictured here was taken from the bottom of a curtain.

Old lace may have rust or mildew stains. Age-old stains are often best left as they are, and fragile pieces of lace should never be treated with bleach or chemicals. To remove rust or iron mould, use a solution of lemon juice and salt. If this does not work, try a proprietary rust-stain remover. Mildew should be soaked in lemon juice or, alternatively, a chloramine-T solution, but only in a well-ventilated area, and the lace should then be rinsed in distilled water.

If you cannot find old lace or would prefer to use new, buy from small independent fabric shops or look in department stores. Cotton lace looks and feels much nicer than synthetic laces. A few manufacturers produce cotton lace in fabric width.

Before you begin the project, cut away any stained or damaged areas from your lace and work out a design to accommodate the remaining pieces. Remember that pieces of lace can be overlapped and any raw or uneven edges turned under. Using a ready-made cotton pillowcase, carefully pin the lace to one layer of the pillowcase. The lace can be pinned in lengths across the width, sewn as a border round the circumference, sewn on the ends as a trim or positioned as a central feature. If desired, work on an ironing board or sleeve board while pinning and stitching the lace in place to avoid sewing through two layers. Use small running or hemming stitches to secure the lace in place. Where lengths join, fold under the raw ends, neatly abut the edges and hand-stitch to secure.

## Appliquéd Feather Blanket

Feathers – both real and imitation – have been used in interior decoration and design for centuries. They are a comforting, natural kind of image and can look stylish as well.

This sumptuous-looking blanket from a charity shop was first dyed a deep grey in the washing machine to felt and colour the blanket. Although dyeing a blanket this way is not normally recommended as it shrinks the wool, the felting that occurs is the desired result for this project. Be sure to use a cool wash to minimize shrinking. If necessary, cut off any satin or bound edging on the blanket and stitch a simple hem to finish the edges.

**2**

**3**

MATERIALS

Light-coloured wool
blanket, a size larger
than that required for
your bed

Charcoal grey
machine dye

Felt pieces in blue, grey
and mauve, or woollen
remnants and machine
dyes in blue and mauve

Pencil and paper

Sewing thread in grey,
blue and mauve

**one**   Dye the wool blanket charcoal grey in the washing machine on a very cool cycle, according to the manufacturer's instructions for cotton. Dye other woollen remnants, if using, in various shades of blue and mauve. Lay the pieces flat and leave to dry thoroughly. If necessary, when dry, press the blanket and remnants with a cool iron.

**two**   Draw a freehand feather design onto a sheet of paper or copy or photocopy one from an art or wallpaper book to the required size. On this blanket, 80 feather shapes, measuring 20 cm (8 in) in length, were used. Cut out a paper template, pin to the fabric and draw round. Cut out the feather shape. Repeat as many times as required.

**three**   Pin the cut-out feather shapes onto the blanket, making sure the colours are evenly distributed and the feathers lie at different angles. Here a collection is concentrated at the bottom of the blanket to look as if the feathers have fallen in a pile. More feathers are spaced out at the top and the middle of the blanket to look as though they are floating down.

**four**   Machine-stitch down the centre of each feather with a close zigzag stitch. This will allow the feathers to curl at the edges, creating movement to the blanket. Here some of the feathers were sewn with thread in a corresponding colour, while others were sewn with an alternative colour.

# Leaf Border

To create a leaf border, cut out leaf shapes from a pale green dyed blanket, as for the Appliquéd Feather Blanket on the facing page. Sew them in a row along the top edge of a cream-coloured blanket, using quite large running stitches, worked in a darker green embroidery thread (floss). Stitch a central vein along the middle of each leaf.

# Pebble Blanket

Hem a length of dark grey fleece using running stitches and a light grey embroidery thread. Decorate the throw with pebble motifs, made by cutting out light grey squares and then rounding the corners. Pin the shapes all over the blanket. Hand-sew in place using running stitches and light grey embroidery thread (floss). To finish the design, sew or tie a flat pebble button in the centre of each shape, leaving the ends hanging as part of the decoration.

## Hot Water Bottle Cover

Hot water bottles are enjoying a style renaissance at the moment and it is not difficult to see why. They provide a warm, wrapped-up comfort in bed and something reassuring to cuddle, especially when made in layers of soft, thick felt. A simple, universal motif – the heart – decorates this cover, but you could easily choose a different motif or even stitch a child's name or initials in a contrasting colour (page 49 provides a chart of initials to be embroidered in cross-stitch).

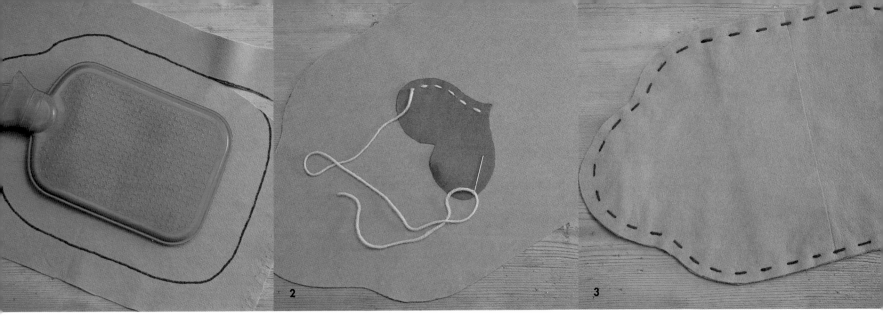

2

3

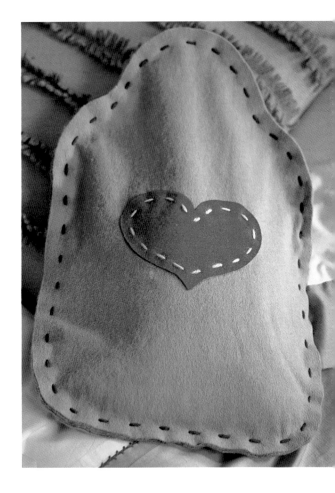

**MATERIALS**

Hot water bottle

Grey felt 1 m (39 in) square

Basting thread

Small square of pink felt

1 skein pale grey tapestry yarn

1 skein bright pink tapestry yarn

Embroidery needle

**one**   Fold the felt in half. For the front, place the hot water bottle on the felt with the top near the fold. Draw round it, adding 4 cm (1¹/₂ in) all round. Cut out the shape from the double thickness of felt and baste the two thicknesses together round the edges. For the back, make a paper template by drawing round the front. Cut the paper in half crosswise. Place each half on the double thickness of felt and cut out, adding 4 cm (1¹/₂ in) to each half at the cut edge. The two half sections will overlap to make the centre back opening. For each piece, baste the two thicknesses together around the edges.

**two**   Cut out a heart shape from pink felt. Using grey tapestry yarn and a running stitch, sew the heart to the centre front of the front cover.

**three**   Lay the front face down on a table. Place the two back pieces on top, overlapping them so that the outer edges are even with those of the front. Pin all round the edges. Fill the hot water bottle with cold water and insert it into the cover through the back opening, checking that it will fit easily. Using a running stitch and pink tapestry yarn, hand-sew the front cover to the back, 1 cm (¹/₂ in) from the edge.

# Felt Rug

Soft felt in muted colours makes a comfortable rug for beside the bed, providing comfort underfoot. The rug will add warmth to wood or tile floors but also looks good on a light-coloured wall-to-wall carpet where it adds visual interest and works to layer textures. The amount of fabric can be adjusted according to the size of rug you desire – here we have made a rug measuring 89 x 221 cm (35 x 87 in). Although we have used rectangles, you could just as easily use squares in two contrasting colours.

### MATERIALS

Two felt pieces in each
of four muted colours,
such as air force blue,
pale grey, lilac and
wisteria, each one
measuring 89 x 56 cm
(35 x 22 in)

Blue sewing thread

Interlining, measuring
82 x 214 cm
(32 x 84 in)

Blue tapestry yarn

Embroidery needle

**one**   Pin and machine-stitch the air force blue
piece of felt to the pale grey along one long side,
using a 1 cm ($^1/_2$ in) seam allowance. Open out and
pin and stitch the other long edge of the pale grey
piece to the lilac piece. In the same way attach the
other edge of the lilac piece to the wisteria-
coloured piece. You should now have a long,
rectangular rug shape. Carefully press open the
seams and topstitch them.

**two**   Repeat step 1 with the remaining four felt
pieces to create the underside of the rug.

**three**   Sandwich the interlining centrally between
the two long felt rug shapes, placed so the right
sides face out. Pin through all thicknesses. Using
blue tapestry yarn and a running stitch, hand-sew
the top to the bottom of the rug just catching the
interlining in the stitches.

# Button Throw

A small item such as a button can evoke warm and happy memories of the clothing or item it originally appeared on. Nearly everyone has a button collection tucked away in a box and, at last, here is a way of using it. This project is easy and yet highly effective, as it does not involve making anything, only embellishing. Choose the buttons carefully. If they are very old, make sure that they are colourfast – traditionally antique buttons had to be taken off every time a garment was washed. If in doubt, sew the button to a piece of cloth and put it through the washing machine to check if it has dyed the fabric beneath.

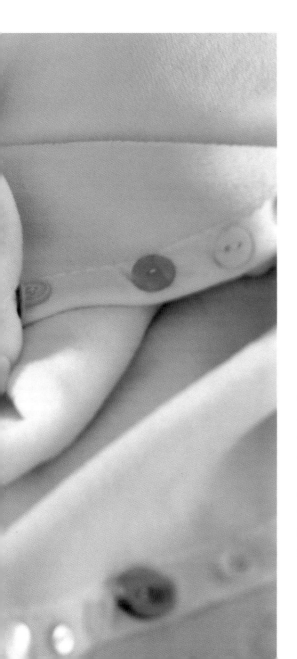

Thrift shops and jumble (rummage) sales are good sources for buttons. Simply buy old clothes and cut off the buttons. Alternatively, ask family members or friends for spare buttons. Select buttons that fit in with your colour palette. Here cream, white and glass buttons combine with the odd blue, pink or brown one to give a hint of colour.

To make the throw, first choose a blanket or throw that has a bound edge in a contrasting texture or colour to the rest of the blanket. Arrange the buttons along the edge to see how they look next to each other. Try spacing them at different intervals and interspersing lines of round buttons with more unusually shaped ones. Using the edge as a guide, sew on the buttons through one layer of the binding only, so that no stitching shows on the reverse side.

## Child's Duvet Cover
This duvet cover, made in a tiny print of blue Viyella, has specially designed flaps at the sides and the bottom which can be slipped under the mattress so that the child can be tucked in for the night, solving the age-old problem of cold, sleepless nights for both the mother and infant. Viyella or soft brushed cotton make ideal comfort fabrics for children's (or even adults') bedding as they are so soft to the touch and feel instantly cosy.

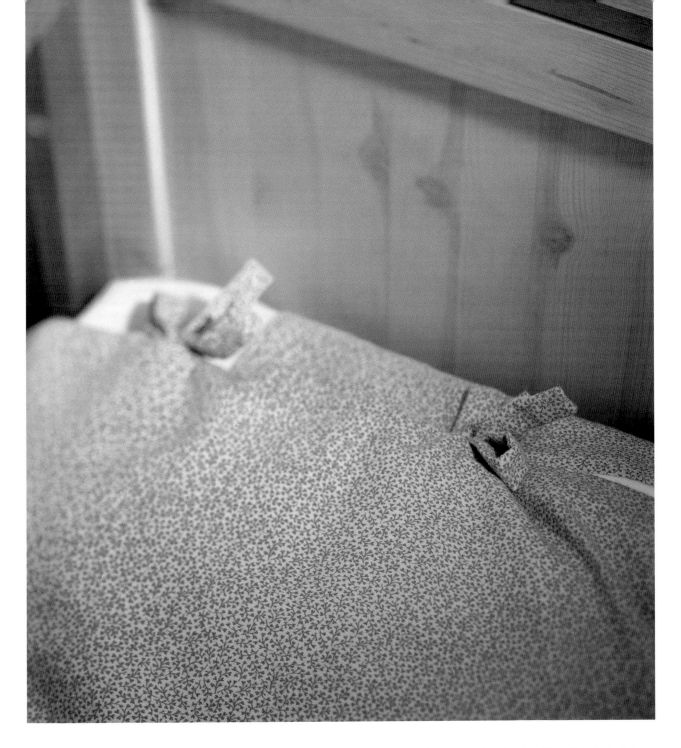

Make fabric ties for the bottom of the duvet cover. This is the prettiest fastening, but if you feel the look is too fussy, use snap fasteners or buttons. Make sure the ties are out of the reach of the baby. This finished cot-sized duvet cover measures 117 x 126 cm (46 x 50 in), but you could easily adapt the size to suit your child's bed – for example, a smaller version for a baby's moses basket, or larger ones for children's bunk beds. Do remember, however, that thick blankets or duvets are not suitable for young babies under 12 months.

7

8

**MATERIALS**

1.5 m (59 in) of 228 cm
(90 in) wide fabric in
soft Viyella or
wincyette sheeting

1.2 m (47 in) of 135 cm
(54 in) wide fabric in a
contrasting pattern

Sewing thread in the
colour of the fabric

**one**  From the 1.5 m (59 in) length of fabric, cut a front measuring 120 x 129 cm (47 x 51 in). Cut three flaps, two of which measure 31 x 99 cm (12 x 39 in) and one which measures 28 x 66 cm (11 x 26 in). From the excess fabric, cut 10 lengths for the ties, each measuring 5 x 32 cm (2 x 12$^{1}/_{2}$ in). From the contrast fabric cut a back piece measuring 120 x 129 cm (47 x 51 in).

**two**  Turn under, press and machine-stitch a narrow 1cm ($^{1}/_{2}$ in) hem on one long and two short sides on the long flaps, and on all four sides of the small flap. Turn under, press and machine-stitch a large 2.5 cm (1 in) double hem on one short side of the front and the back pieces.

**three**  Lay the back piece right side up with the hemmed end at the bottom. Position the front piece wrong side up on top, with the hemmed end at the bottom and the edges even. Pin and machine-stitch together along the top edge, using a 1 cm ($^{1}/_{2}$ in) seam allowance (this seam will have no flap or opening).

**four**  Sandwich the two large flaps between the front and back pieces so that the right sides of the flaps face up and the long outer raw edges of the front, back and flaps are even. (The flaps do not project beyond the front and back at this stage.) Position the flaps so they are 15 mm ($^{5}/_{8}$ in) from the bottom (hemmed) edge. Pin in place along both side seams. Machine-stitch through all three thicknesses, using 1 cm ($^{1}/_{2}$ in) seam allowances.

**five**  Using a 1 cm ($^{1}/_{2}$ in) seam allowance, pin and machine-stitch along the bottom, from each side corner for a distance of 16 cm (6$^{1}/_{4}$ in), being careful not to catch the flap in the seam. Turn the duvet cover right sides out, poking out the four corners, and press.

**six** Make the ties by folding each fabric strip in half lengthwise with wrong sides together. Turn under, press and pin all raw edges to enclose them within the strip. Neatly machine-stitch as close as possible to the turned-in edges.

**seven** Place five ties at regular intervals across the opening, pinning the ends to the wrong side of the front. Machine-stitch in place along the hem on the front, without stitching through the back.

**eight** Pin the remaining flap centrally on the bottom hem of the back on the right side. One long edge should be aligned with the hem and the flap should project beyond the cover. Pin the remaining five ties along this edge to match up with the front piece ties (three of the ties will be pinned on top of the flap and the other two at either side). Machine-stitch along the hem to attach the ties and flap.

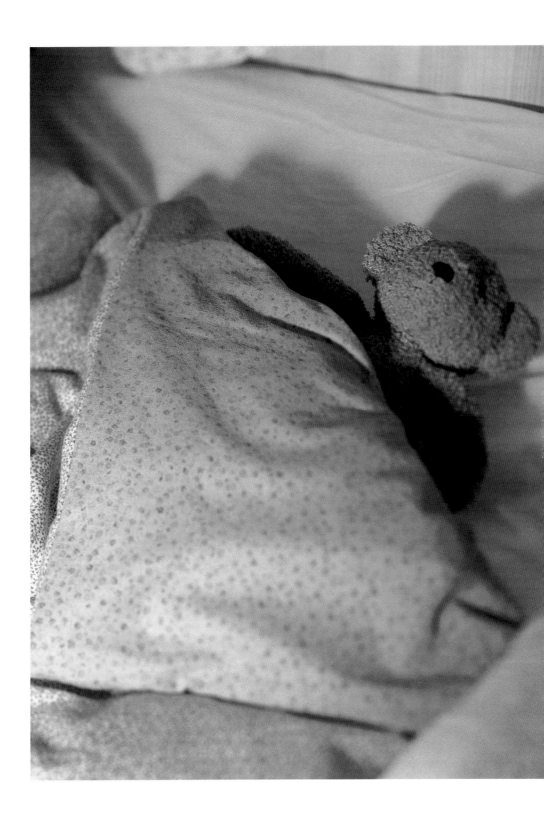

## Monogrammed Baby Blanket
Nostalgia plays a large part in comfort and it is often the handmade gifts that evoke fond memories of childhood and end up being passed down through the generations. One such wonderful gift is a monogrammed baby blanket, perfect as a special gift for a newborn baby or for a christening present.

Buy cashmere or another soft, non-itchy fabric for this project. Fleece is another good choice as it is so easy to launder. For binding the edges, good

haberdashery (notions) stores sell blanket ribbon which is cut on the bias and folded down its length. Made in satin, it comes in many soft colours,

such as pale yellow, blue, pink, cream and white.

MATERIALS

1 m (39 in) of soft fine
fleece or cashmere, at
least 80 cm (32 in) wide

4 m (4¹/₃ yd) narrow
pale blue satin bias,
specially made for
blankets (see page 47)

Pale blue sewing thread

1 skein pale blue
embroidery thread
(floss) (DMC blue 3753)

Embroidery hoop
and needle

Tissue paper and
gift box

**one** Cut the fabric so it measures 1 m x 80 cm (39 x 32 in). Cut the corners into a curve to make the blanket edges look softer.

**two** With right sides together, pin and stitch the bias binding to the raw edge of fleece or cashmere, round the entire circumference. At the corners, ease the binding round the curve for smooth edges. On stretch fabric, stitch by hand. Gently press the seam and fold the binding to the reverse side to enclose the raw edge. Pin and stitch in place with the edge turned under.

**three** Pick out your chosen initials from the alphabet chart on the right. Mark the position for the initials on the blanket and stretch the fabric over an embroidery hoop. Starting at the central point of the middle letter and using three strands of embroidery thread (floss), cross-stitch the letters (see Cross-stitch Pillowcase, page 27), following the chart given. If you are not comfortable working freehand, baste a piece of fine waste canvas into position to use as a guide (see page 29), removing it thread by thread afterwards. Wrap the finished blanket in layers of tissue paper and place in a beautiful satin-finish gift box.

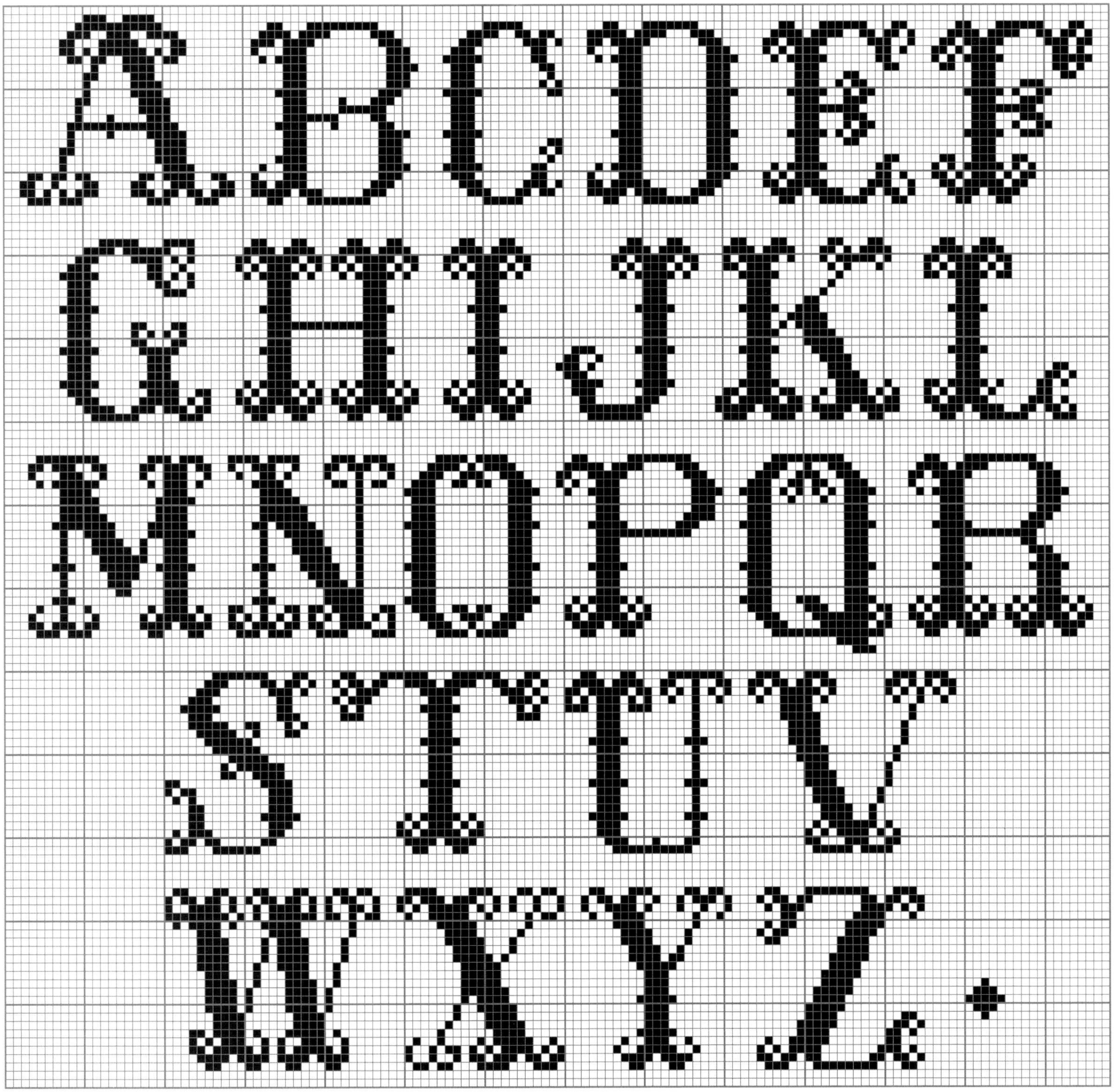

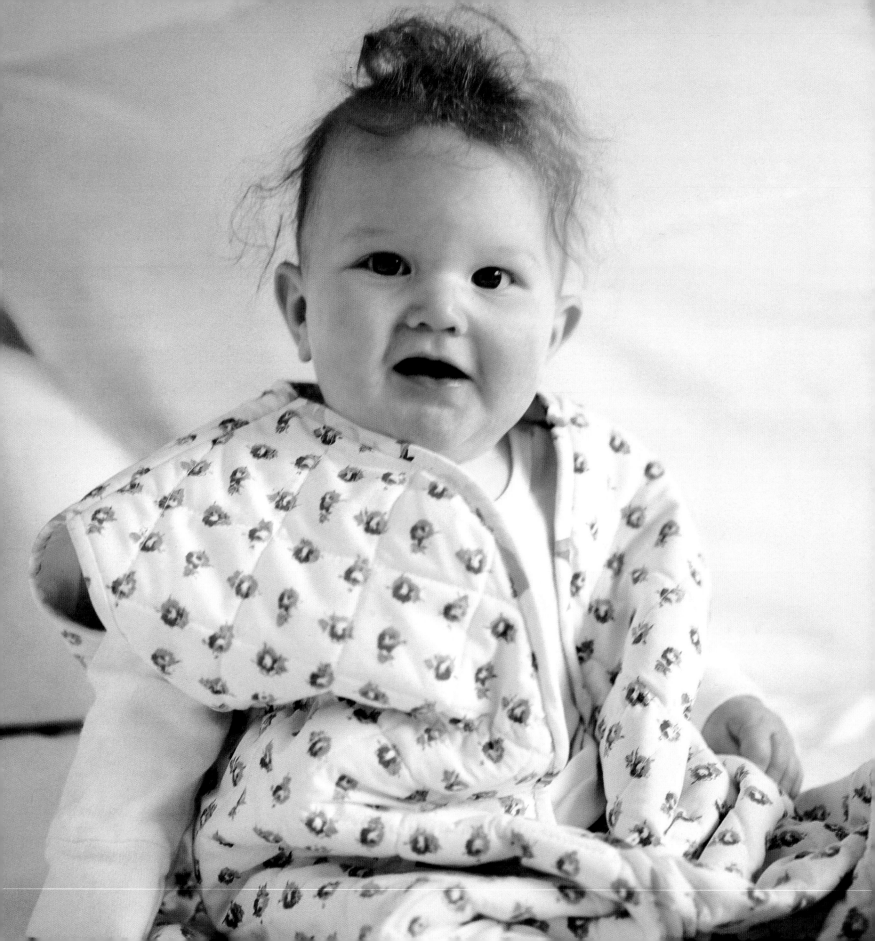

# Baby Sleeping Bag

If you have ever suffered sleepless nights because your baby wakes up feeling cold after kicking off blankets and duvets in the middle of the night, you will love this idea. Although these baby sleeping bags are available in some shops, they usually retail at a hefty price. The bag is an ideal way to keep a baby warm while still allowing him or her to kick and move about. When the baby has grown too large to sleep in the bag, open up the bottom seam and continue to use it as a dressing gown. You may prefer to buy ready-quilted fabric for this project, rather than quilt your own.

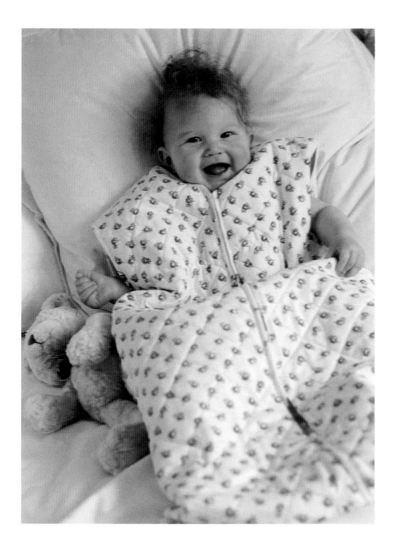

*A warm baby is a happy one! This quilted sleeping bag is perfect for keeping a wriggling baby snug and warm. To prevent the sleeping bag rucking up around the baby's neck, a band of elastic is sewn around the middle of the bag.*

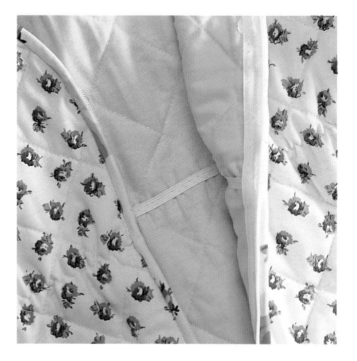

Zipper starts here

Elastic here                    Elastic here

Dart

BABY SLEEPING BAG

Cut 1 on fold

Place on fold

Centre back

Centre front

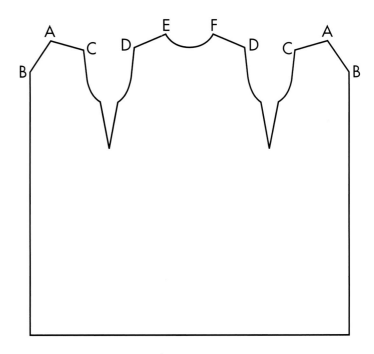

*Scale: one square in this pattern*

*represents a 5 cm (2 in) square*

*on gridded pattern paper.*

**M A T E R I A L S**

Two 1 m (39 in) squares of
cotton print fabric

One 1 m (39 in) square of
100 g (4 oz) wadding
(batting)

5 cm (2 in) gridded pattern
paper and pencil

Sewing thread in the colours
of the fabric

3 m (3$^1/_3$ yd) of 13 mm
($^1/_2$ in) wide bias binding in
a contrasting fabric, or make
your own (see step three)

60 cm ($^2/_3$ yd) of 5 mm
($^1/_4$ in) elastic

One 51 cm (20 in) closed-
end zipper

**one** Sandwich the layer of wadding (batting) between the two fabric squares (right sides facing out) and pin together. Mark criss-crossed diagonal stitching lines at even intervals all over the piece and machine-stitch along the lines. If the fabric has a large-scale printed design, such as flowers, leaves or geometric shapes, you may like to outline the design with machine-stitching to quilt. Always sew in the same direction, as the quilting will be more even this way.

**two** Transfer the pattern on the facing page onto gridded pattern paper to the scale given, copying the pattern shape square by square and cut out. Fold the quilted fabric in half with wrong sides together. Position the pattern with the centre back on the fold and pin in place. Cut out the fabric. Do not cut along the foldline.

**three** To make the bias binding, cut the fabric on the diagonal into strips 2.5 cm (1 in) wide. To join the strips, place one end on top of another at right angles, right sides together. Machine-stitch together, as close to the edge as possible. Open out and press the seam flat.

**four** With right sides together, machine-stitch both sets of darts using a running stitch. Open out the sleeping bag and machine-stitch the bias binding round both raw edges at the front (from A to the lower edge), neatly overlapping it at the ends (see Hooded Bath Towel, page 125).

**five** Bind the armholes from C to D on both sides. Bind the neck from E to F.

**six** With right sides together, machine-stitch the shoulder seams (AC to DE and FD to CA) to join, using a 5 mm ($^1/_4$ in) seam allowance.

**seven** Pin each end of the elastic in place on the wrong side of the fabric, as shown on the pattern. Hand-sew along the length of the elastic with a running stitch.

**eight** Turn the bag the right side out. Pin the left centre front seam slightly over the right centre front seam, overlapping by about the width of the binding. Sew up this seam 30 cm (11$^3/_4$ in) from the bottom of the bag. Insert the zipper from the V neck to the top of the seam you have just sewn. Close the bottom edge of the bag by overlocking or using a zigzag stitch. This will allow the bottom seam to be opened up later on, so the bag can be used as a dressing gown.

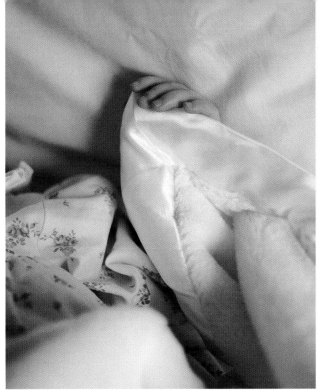 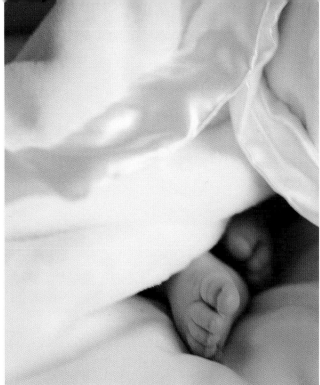

# Comfort Blanket

Although a comfort blanket is almost a cliché, many children love to have a blanket to cuddle when feeling tired or upset, so why not make it beautiful? A good idea is to make two identical blankets and alternate them when one needs washing.

**MATERIALS**

Two pieces machine-washable cream fleece fabric, measuring 70 x 100 cm (27$^1$/$_2$ x 39 in)

4 m (4$^1$/$_3$ yd) of 10 cm (4 in) wide machine-washable cream satin

Cream sewing thread

**one** With wrong sides together, pin and stitch the two pieces of fleece together round all sides, using a 1 cm ($^1$/$_2$ in) seam allowance.

**two** Fold and press the satin in half lengthwise, wrong sides together. In the same way as sewing bias binding, pin the satin onto one long edge of the fleece with right sides together, leaving 1 cm ($^1$/$_2$ in) of excess at the end. Sew down the long side, stopping 1 cm ($^1$/$_2$ in) from the second edge, leaving 5 cm (2 in) of satin hanging. Repeat with the other three sides, leaving excess satin to hang at each corner. Press open the seams.

**three** To mitre the corners, pull the two ends of the satin strips so the right sides are facing each other; pin evenly together along the outside raw edges. Stitch together from the end of the stitching in the corner to the outside edge of the satin at an angle of 45°. Trim the excess and press open the diagonal seam.

**four** Open out and press the seam using a low heat. Fold the satin binding over to the reverse side of the blanket to enclose all raw edges. Turn under a hem on the binding and pin in place. Fold the corners to mitre them, pinning in place. Hand-sew the satin to the fleece with hemming stitch.

living rooms

# A living room

is a public, as well as a private, space. Because of this, many people tend to decorate their living areas like an old 19th-century parlour, a room which is kept for 'best' and tends towards formality. But what one really requires from a living room is comfort, a place to entertain friends easily, without guests feeling that they have to be on their best behaviour. The room should be easy on the eye, in colours that harmonize. Use matt paint on the walls and eggshell, rather than shiny gloss, on the woodwork. For reasons of practicality, the paint finishes and furnishings should be hardwearing and easy to clean, especially if you have children. Sofas should be large, inviting and covered in throws and cushions. What could be nicer than to curl up on a comfortable sofa with a good book in front of an open fire?

Remember, too, that a room can be dual-purpose. Incorporate clever storage ideas for children's toys so the room can be transformed from a play area in the afternoon to an adult setting in the evening. Use a rustic wicker hamper or a wooden Shaker box to store toys, or hide a computer behind fitted cupboards or an antique wooden screen partition. To prevent the living room looking like a public meeting place, fill it with objects that reflect your personality, such as objets d'art, collections of china, or paintings and photographs of your family.

Although you do not need to change the entire room with the seasons, do adapt accessories, textiles and cushions. For winter choose warm wools and felt for furnishings. Cushions can be made from old sweaters or dyed and felted blankets. Curtains of velvet or suede can be hung. For summer, choose curtains in lightweight voile or linen and embellish them with embroidery or beads. A favourite sari or silk scarf can be made into a cushion or wall hanging. As well as looking good, your surroundings should feel good. Try using tactile materials and, as a final touch, do not forget to fill the room with enticing aromas, whether from a bowl of potpourri, cut flowers or even a jug of fresh herbs.

A collection of soft and welcoming cushions in a variety of knitted fabrics bring comfort to a sofa. Some are made from old sweaters (see page 70), while others have been specially knitted as cushion covers.

# Fake Fur Throws

Fake fur has had a poor reputation, mainly because of acrylic versions in lurid pinks, greens and oranges. There are, however, some very beautiful and good-quality imitation furs, which are warm, snuggly and the perfect thing to wrap up in on a cold night. They are available in a variety of colours and finishes, such as bearskin, leopardskin and even longhairs in unusual blue-grey and turquoise shades.

Quality imitation fur throws are expensive, so you will make a considerable saving by sewing your own. Most fake furs come in wide widths, making them ideal for throws or bedcovers. Always remember to make sure the pile goes in the same direction when joining fur pieces. Choose the best lining you can afford. Here a heavyweight slipper satin was used to line the bearskin throw and a white cotton velvet lines the leopardskin throw on page 64.

*Contrasts of colour and texture combine to make a beautiful and comforting fake fur throw to banish the chill of winter evenings.*

## Trimmed Furs

Lined lengths of fake fur look luxurious when finished with an edging in a natural or heavily textured fabric, such as suede or leather fringing, a deep-pile velvet ribbon or even a punched suede trim. A length of rope trim makes another interesting contrast to fur.

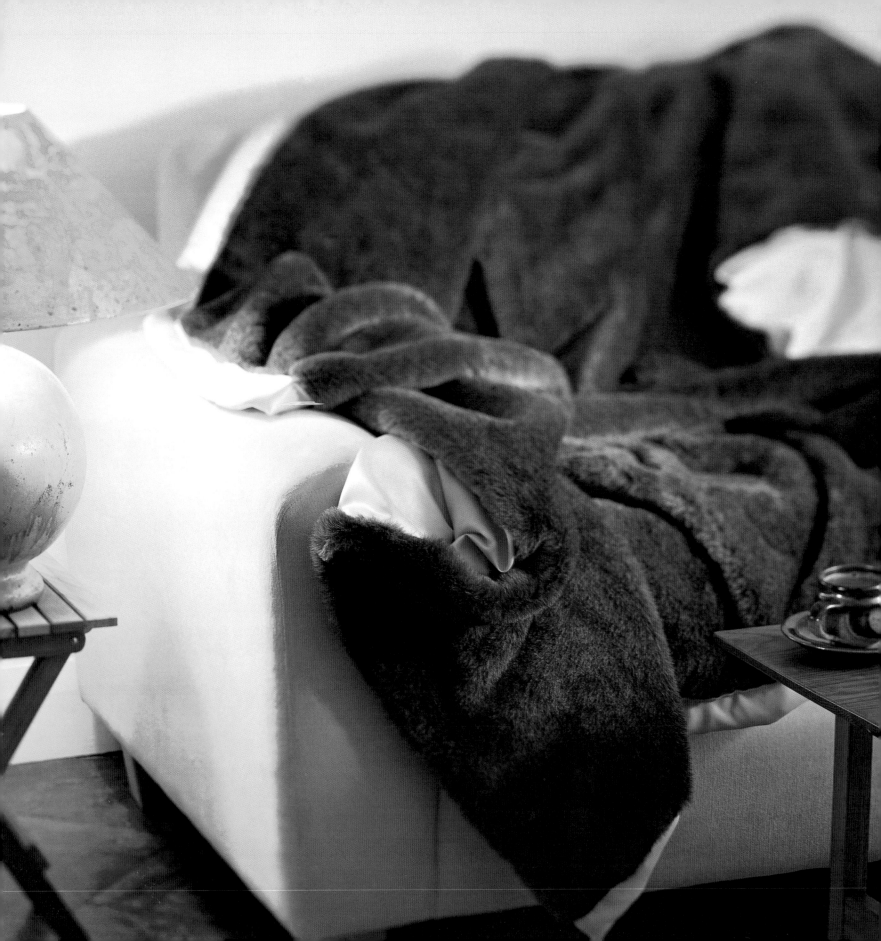

# Satin-edged Bearskin Throw

This has to be the ultimate in decadent luxury – a rich, deep brown fur throw lined with smooth cream satin. The combination of textures makes this throw sheer heaven to snuggle under on a chilly evening. As well as using it to dress up a plain sofa, this throw would work equally well on a bed.

**MATERIALS**

2.7 m (3 yd) of 150 cm (60 in) wide fake bearskin fur

5.5 m (6 yd) of 90 cm (35 in) wide heavyweight slipper satin lining

Sewing thread in the colours of the fur and lining

**one**  Cut the satin lining into two pieces, each measuring 2.7 m (3 yd) long. With right sides together, sew the two lengths together along one long side using a 1 cm ($^1/_2$ in) seam allowance, to make a piece approximately 178 cm (69 in) wide.

**two**  With the right sides together, fold the lining in half along the seamline and cut away 8 cm (3 in) from the outer edge of both thicknesses of the fabric. The width will now be 162 cm (63 in).

**three**  With right sides together, place the lining on top of the fake fur, aligning the short raw edges. Using a ballpoint needle on the sewing machine, pin and stitch down each long side using a 1 cm ($^1/_2$ in) seam allowance.

**four**  Smooth out the lining to centre it on top of the fur. Pin the bottom centre of the lining to the bottom centre width of the fur. Pin outwards along the bottom edge, making sure the excess that creates the side borders is exactly the same on both sides. At the edges of the throw you will be pinning satin onto satin. Machine-stitch along this seam from corner to corner. Turn right sides out.

**five**  Smooth out the lining. Turn under and press 5 mm ($^1/_4$ in) on each long edge of the lining, then fold the lining over the edge of the fur to make a neat bound edge. Pin through all thicknesses from the right side of the throw. Along the top open edge, turn under the remaining raw edges of the fur and lining and close the gap with slipstitch.

**six**  Finally, topstitch along each long side, where the satin border joins the fake fur and as close to the fur as possible. Use a pin to pull out any fur caught in the edges of the seams.

# Leopardskin Throw

In contrast to the bearskin on the previous pages, this throw does not have an edging – the leopardskin pattern is distinctive enough without it. The white velvet lining provides a striking contrast to the strong pattern.

To make the throw, cut a length of white velvet to the same measurement as a length of leopardskin fake fur. With right sides together, machine-stitch round three and a half sides. Turn right side out. Pin and stitch the gap closed using a hemming stitch. Carefully press the seams on the lining side with the iron on a low setting.

# Fur Cushions

Furry cushions in vibrant shades of blue and green add a fun, contemporary accent to neutral interiors. Fake fur cushions can be made from remnants leftover from throws or other projects. Simply fold over a rectangular length of fur so the right sides are together and sew up the side seams. Turn right side out, insert the cushion pad and close the opening with a neat hemming stitch.

## Embroidered Felt Cushions

These stylish contemporary felt cushions are made from pieced patches of dyed wool, embellished with simple embroidered designs and old mother-of-pearl buttons. Knitting yarn or embroidery thread (floss) can be dyed to match the fabric by placing it in an old pair of tights, knotting the top, and dyeing it with the fabric in the washing machine. Make a collection of cushions using the same fabrics but in different combinations and in varied designs.

*Different finishes for cushions: organdy ribbon held in place by mother-of-pearl buttons; heart-shaped soapstone buttons with tiny rocaille beads; oversewn raffia and string; narrow bands of silk and velvet ribbon in shades of green.*

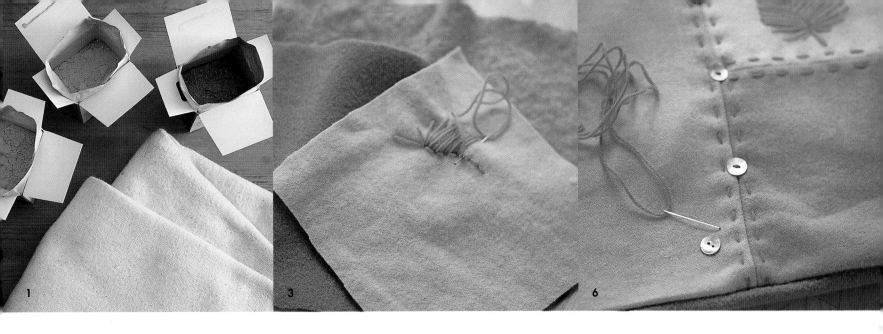

## MATERIALS

50 x 78 cm (20 x 31 in) woollen fabric, or a small wool blanket

Machine dyes in three colours, such as violet, pink and grey

Double knitting yarn (sport yarn) or embroidery thread (floss) in pastel colours

Embroidery needle

Sewing thread to match dye colours

Mother-of-pearl buttons

35 cm (14 in) cushion pad

**one**  Follow the dye manufacturer's instructions for dyeing cotton. Cut the blanket or fabric into three pieces so each piece can be dyed a different colour (step two gives the finished sizes for each colour). Wet the fabric and then place it in the washing machine with the dye and salt, as instructed. Do a separate dye batch for each colour required. Remove the fabric pieces, lay flat and allow to dry.

**two**  Cut two squares in two different colours, each measuring 20 cm (8 in) square. Cut a rectangle in a third colour, measuring 20 x 38 cm (8 x 15 in). Cut two back pieces measuring 30 x 38 cm (12 x 15 in).

**three**  Using one strand of knitting yarn or three strands of embroidery thread (floss), embroider a feather design onto one of the squares. Sketch out the design freehand with a pencil first, if desired, and then embroider the straight stitches that make up the shape. Stitch a line of close running stitches down the centre to define the shape.

**four**  With right sides together and using a 1 cm ($^1/_2$ in) seam allowance, sew the square with the feather to the square without the feather along one side to create a rectangle, making sure you position the feather correctly. With right sides facing, stitch this piece to the rectangle along one long side, again using a 1 cm ($^1/_2$ in) seam allowance, to create a 38 cm (15 in) square cushion front.

**five**  Carefully press open the seams and, working from the right side, hand-stitch two even lines of running stitches on either side of each seam using knitting yarn or embroidery thread (floss).

**six**  On one long side of each back piece, turn under, pin and machine-stitch a double 2.5 cm (1 in) hem. Overlap the two back pieces at the hemmed edges so they make a 38 cm (15 in) square. Pin to the front with right sides together. Machine-stitch around all four edges using a 1.5 cm ($^1/_3$ in) seam allowance. Turn right side out. Sew mother-of-pearl buttons down the centre front seam to finish and insert the cushion pad.

## Sweater Cushions

Before you throw away a much-loved sweater which may have seen better days, why not recycle it? Simply cut away any damaged areas, such as moth-holes, frayed sleeves or worn elbows. Choose sweaters with interesting stitching or patterns, such as the Fair Isle design used here. Make features of button fronts, such as on this cardigan. For a felted look, wash the fabrics in a hot cycle in the washing machine. The size of the finished cushion will depend on the usable surface area of the sweater.

One of the cushions shown here is made from a fawn-coloured mohair sweater, cut and sewn as a square, with a pale pink mohair shrug knotted round the front to add interest. A larger cushion has been made from a cotton knit dress in ice grey-blue, while a nubbly cardigan has been turned into a front-opening cushion.

MATERIALS

A sweater with a surface
area larger than the
cushion pad

Sewing thread

Cushion pad

**one** Wash the sweaters before turning them into cushions. If you want them to be felted, wash them on a hot cycle. Otherwise, wash by hand using soap flakes.

**two** Centre the cushion pad onto the area of the sweater you want to use as a feature, ensuring that any pattern or design is squared up. Measure and cut out one square of fabric about 2.5 cm (1 in) larger all round than the cushion pad. Cut out two rectangles the same width as the front square but only two-thirds the length.

**three** Using a ballpoint needle on the sewing machine, machine-stitch all raw edges with a zigzag stitch to prevent unravelling.

**four** Turn under, pin and stitch a double 2.5 cm (1 in) hem on one long side of each rectangle (these sides will form the overlapping ends for the envelope-style back opening).

**five** With right sides together, pin the two back pieces to the front piece so the raw edges are even, overlapping the hemmed edges of the back piece. Machine-stitch the back pieces to the front piece around all four edges, using a 1 cm ($^1/_2$ in) seam allowance. Turn right side out and insert the cushion pad.

# Fabric Cushions

The cushions here have been made from old clothes and fabric remnants in muted, subtle colours that look good when arranged together on a sofa or tucked into an armchair. A blouse, a shirt, an old tie–dyed silk scarf, a pair of jeans and pieces of blue–dyed linen and silk have been used. Two of these cushions have used the original button openings on the blouse fronts for inserting and removing the cushion pad. The faded denim cushion uses a seam on the jeans as a decorative feature. As with the sweater cushions featured on the previous pages,

*These feminine cushions in gentle shades of blue have been designed to make the most of soft faded prints, button detailing and frills.*

each garment needs to be checked carefully for holes and any stains that cannot be washed out. Darts may need to be unstitched to make the fabric

square (although the fabric inside the dart may not have faded to the same degree) or trims may need to be cut off. Always wash and press the fabrics

before cutting out the cushion cover pieces. Jumble sales and thrift shops are good sources of old clothes if you don't have anything suitable in your

own wardrobe.

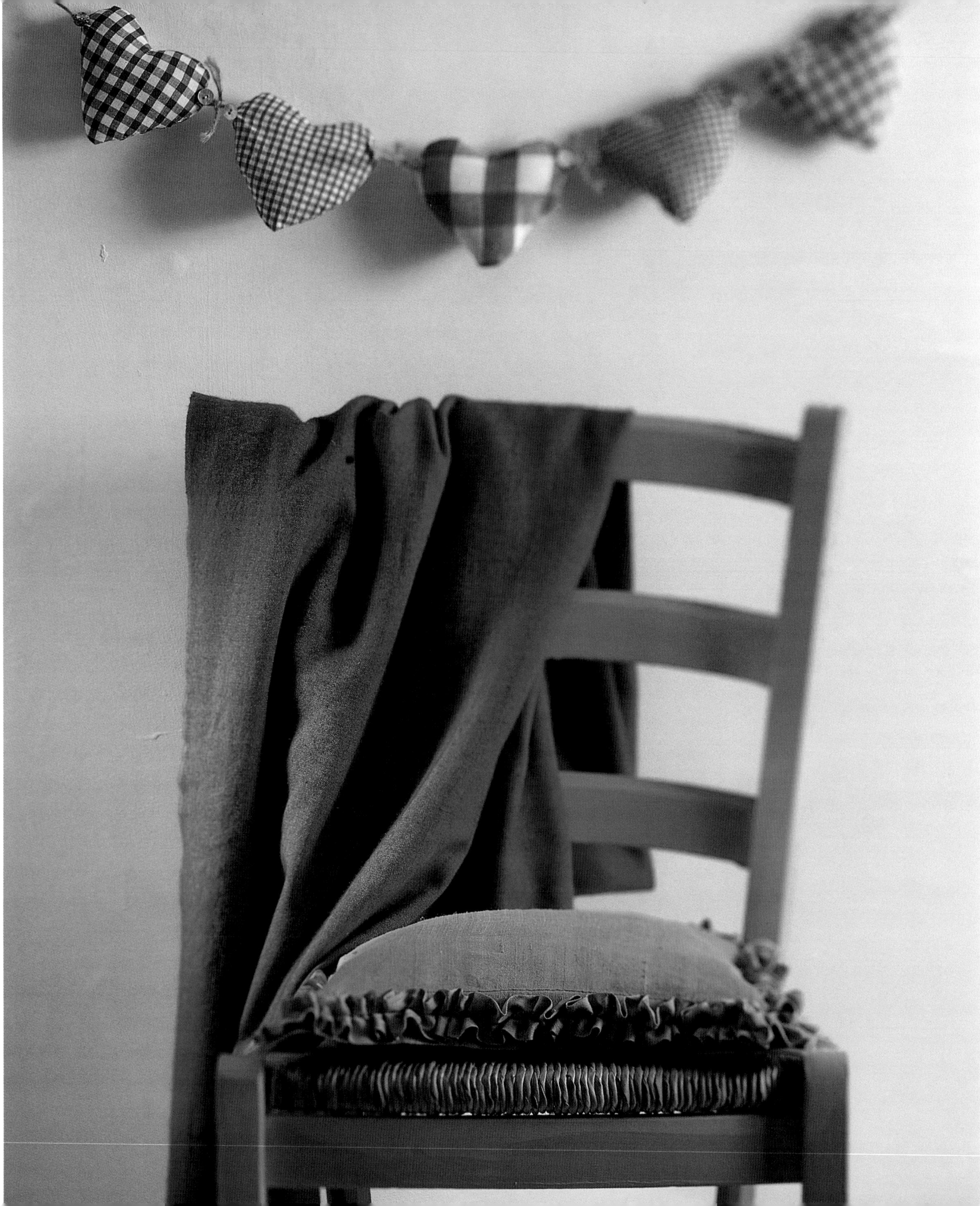

# Silk Frilly-edged Cushion

**MATERIALS**

1.2 m (1¹/₃ yd) pale
blue silk dupion

Pale blue sewing thread

30 cm (12 in)
cushion pad

**one**  From the silk dupion, cut one 38 cm (15 in) square and two rectangles measuring 24 x 38 cm (9¹/₂ x 15 in). Cut a long strip measuring 8 x 120 cm (3¹/₄ x 47 in).

**two**  Turn under, pin and machine-stitch a narrow double hem at one long side of each rectangle.

**three**  With right sides together, position the two rectangles on the square piece with the hemmed edges overlapping in the centre. Align the raw edges and then pin and machine-stitch the rectangles to the front square round all four sides, using a 1 cm (¹/₂ in) seam allowance.

**four**  Turn right side out and press the cushion cover. Machine-stitch a line of running stitches all round the cushion, 3 cm (1¹/₄ in) from the edge through all the thicknesses.

**five**  Turn under and press both long raw edges of the strip, overlapping them slightly. Stitch a line of gathering stitches up the middle.

**six**  Gather the strip until it fits round the edge of the cushion cover. Pin the frill to the outer edge of the cushion cover and stitch in place along the existing stitching line.

# Chenille Throw

Chenille is another one of those fabrics reminiscent of bygone eras. Time was when all parlours or best rooms would not be complete without a chenille tablecloth topped by an aspidistra plant. Though the colours were harsh in those days, the feel of the cloth was heavy, silky and slippery. Today chenille can be bought on the roll in soft hues of light olive green and heather. Here a light olive throw has been edged with a cream chenille fringe.

To make the throw, buy a piece of chenille as long as it is wide. Turn under, pin and machine-stitch a narrow double hem on each edge. Pin the fringe over the hemmed edges on the right side, folding the corners to mitre as you go. Machine-stitch in place with a running stitch. Using sharp scissors, trim the fringe of straggly ends if necessary.

## Cotton Throws

Heavyweight damask cotton and chain-stitched self-coloured cotton fabric both make pretty summer throws. Choose 100 per cent cotton trims in unbleached, cream or natural tones. Machine-stitch a double hem along all edges before pinning and hand-sewing the trim in place. Choose a good-quality trimming, such as heavyweight fringing woven onto a thick braid or tactile chenille pompoms.

## Suede Curtain

By its very nature a soft and luxurious material, suede feels sensuous against the skin. The contrast between suede and leather is one worth exploring in an interior scheme. Here the muted sage-green suede curtain in the background and the lighter suede cushions in the foreground are set off by a warm brown leather armchair.

Suede can be purchased by the metre or yard. Although quite expensive, once you have purchased a length, you do not have to do anything else to make it into a curtain. The piece can be hung from café clips and does not need lining or interlining as it offers enough insulation. Alternatively, eyelets (grommets) can be punched along the top edge using a do-it-yourself kit, which is an easy method if you follow the instructions. Choose enormous eyelets through which a curtain pole can be pushed. Practise on an offcut first if you are unsure. Another way to hang the curtain is by ribbon or leather thongs tied through smaller eyelets.

Hides can be sewn together to make up a suede curtain. Always choose the best-quality suede that you can afford and choose pieces that are the same thickness and have been tanned in the same manner. With scraps, you may find that the edges are thinner than the rest, but these edges will probably be cut away when you trim the shape to square it up. Make sure the sewing machine is strong enough for the job. Most domestic machines will sew through thin-to-medium skins, but you will need to use a wedge-point leather needle. Because most suedes are not washable, the hide can be cleaned using a suede cleaner, available from most shoe shops.

# Suede Cushions

Suede cushions are back in vogue. They look stylish and feel soft and comforting. They are available to buy in a variety of versatile sizes, from small chair or sofa cushions to enormous beanbags or cubes that you can sink into at the end of the day. Alternatively, it is relatively easy to sew a number of small scatter cushions or large floor cushions yourself – the beauty of these cushions is that they rely on the quality and feel of the suede rather than a complicated design for their sheer good looks.

As with the curtains shown on the previous pages, you will need to use a leather needle to sew your own suede cushions. Depending on the size desired, making a cushion is a good opportunity to create something beautiful from leftover pieces of suede or leather. As with any material with a pile, such as velvet, fake fur or chenille, suede has a nap. Remember that unless the nap is facing the same way on all adjoining pieces, each piece will look very different in the same light. Some sections might appear dark and almost damp while others seem far lighter in colour. Suede can be turned into any style of cushion. However, as it is an expensive material, it is better to fit in a zipper or snap fasteners along one side rather than overlapping the suede to create an envelope-style opening. If making floor cushions, you could make the base in a heavyweight fabric, such as canvas or hessian (burlap).

**Summer Curtains**   Comfort has as much to do with being cool and comfortable in summer as with being warm and cosy in winter. In summer, fabrics such as cotton, voile, linen and even an open-weave hessian (burlap) work well at the windows, gently filtering bright sunlight and creating softly dappled interiors.

Another summery idea is to sew white feathers at regular intervals along a white voile curtain. The feathers look exquisite fluttering gently on a breezy day. The easiest way to attach the feathers is to over-sew the central spine at the base of the feather. You may have to remove a few of the wispy tendrils to prevent the thread becoming tangled in the feather. The tip of the feather remains free to wave in the breeze.

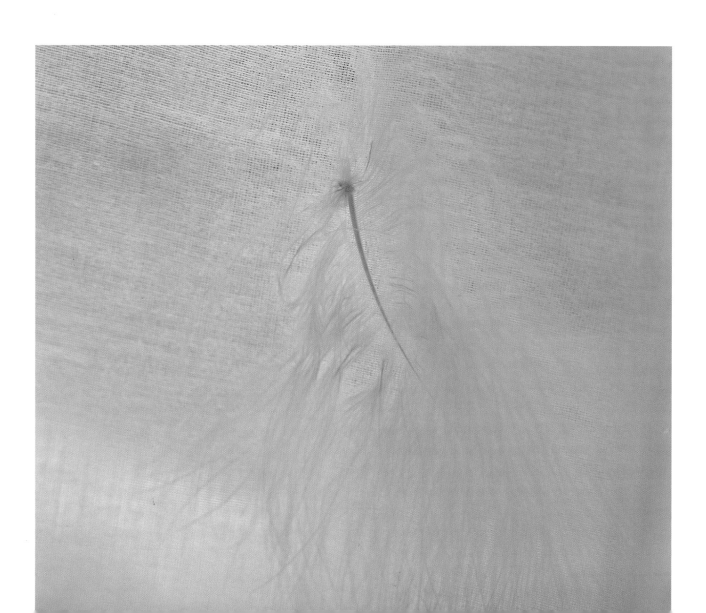

## Fine Linen Curtain

The unusual idea for this elegant pair of curtains was inspired by my daughter's organdy-trimmed linen dress. Here silk dupion is combined with pure white linen for a contrast of textures and fabrics rather than colours. The linen curtains can be purchased ready-made or sewn as simple hemmed panels with a casing or with café clips or tabs along the top for a curtain rod. The design is created by sewing buttonholes at even intervals down the inner edges of the curtains.

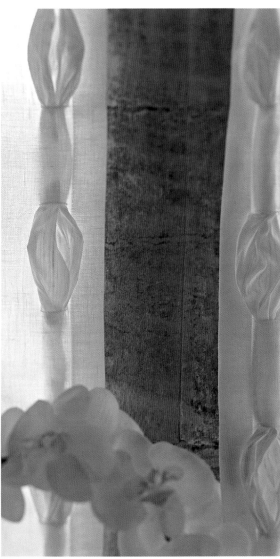

3

4

**MATERIALS**

Two unlined linen curtain panels with a narrow hemmed border to the required size for your window

Two lengths of 17 cm (6¹/₂ in) wide silk dupion, the length measuring 1¹/₄ times the length of the curtain

Interfacing for buttonholes

**one** Measure and mark buttonholes at regular intervals along the length of each curtain at the inner edge. Here we used intervals of 8 cm (3¹/₄ in). Reinforcing with interfacing to give some substance to the buttonholes, stitch each buttonhole as marked.

**two** Using a small pair of scissors with sharp points, carefully cut through each buttonhole to create the opening.

**three** Neatly cut away the excess interfacing around each buttonhole, cutting close to the stitching.

**four** To make a pretty edging, fold the raw edges of the length of silk dupion to the back then thread the dupion through the buttonholes on each curtain. Hand-sew the dupion at the top and bottom of the curtain on the wrong side to secure.

**Rosebud Curtains**  Buy simple white organdy curtains with patch pockets and fill the pockets with dried rosebuds to make a pretty summer curtain. Alternatively, fill the pockets with lavender sprigs for a perfumed room. The curtains are available from most home-ware shops in a range of colours. If you cannot find similar curtains to buy, make your own by cutting organdy squares, folding small hems and sewing onto the curtains as pockets. Use the selvedge of the fabric to act as the upper edge of the pocket, to avoid turning a hem here.

# Linen Border Curtain

Add a heavy linen border to a white voile panel for a fresh-looking window effect. First decide how wide you want the border to be. A smaller curtain can be made to fit a larger window by adding a deep border, or a wide border can create a lush curtain that trails and swoops across the floor. Here we have used a simple panel that is hung by café clips, but you may want to stitch a casing for a curtain rod or a header tape along the top of the finished curtain.

To make this curtain, first measure a voile curtain panel along the length and width. For the border, you will need three strips of linen. Two should measure the length of the curtain plus the depth of the bottom border and one should measure the width of the curtain plus the depth of the side border, plus hems and seam allowances all round.

To make the border, sew the borders along the sides and bottom of the curtain with right sides together and mitring the corners (see Felt-edged Door Curtain, page 94). Press the seam open towards the outside edge, away from the white voile. Turn under, pin and stitch a double hem along the outer raw edges to finish.

# Hessian Print Curtain

A stylized floral pattern of alliums and fritillaries decorates an open-weave hessian (burlap) fabric. Here the fabric colour matches that of the stone window surrounds and the subtle design is etched in a raised brown and white rubberized surface ink. Being lightweight, the curtains have been left unlined to allow the light to shine through and to emphasize the pattern. The curtains are made as simple hemmed panels using a 7.5 cm (3 in) gathered header tape at the top. If you wish, it is possible to decorate a plain piece of hessian yourself. First, draw a design in chalk on the fabric, then go over the outlines using an expanding paint specially developed for home textiles (available from good art suppliers or craft shops).

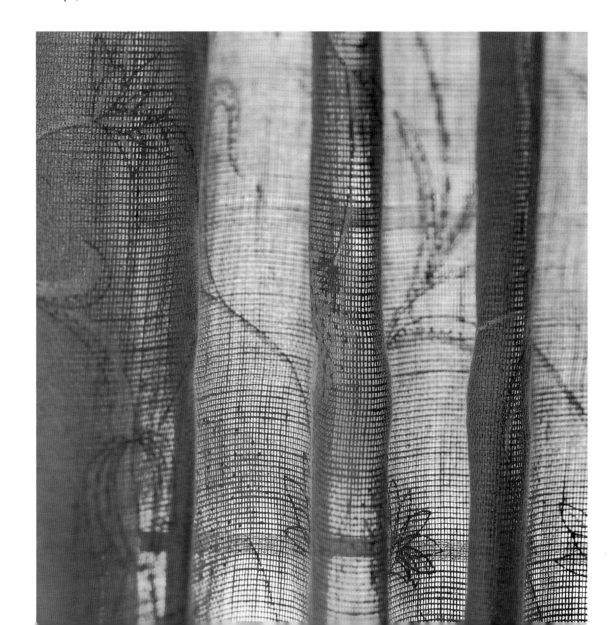

# Felt-edged Door Curtain

A door curtain can be both embellished and enlarged by adding a colourful contrasting trim and a few button details. Here a raspberry-pink edging and pink covered buttons have been added to a rust-brown tab-topped velvet curtain. Using a double thickness of felt makes a more heavyweight material, which will help keep the hallway cosy and draught-free. Make the curtain about 30 cm (12 in) longer than the door so that it can fall onto the floor, preventing draughts creeping in at ankle level. This curtain hangs on a door rod that is specially designed to swing the curtain back as the door opens.

**MATERIALS**
Pink felt (see measurements below)
Rust-brown ready-made unlined velvet curtain
Tacking thread in a contrasting colour
Pink and rust-brown sewing thread
Self-covering buttons

**one** To work out the amount of felt needed, add up the total measurements of the border, as described below, doubling it to allow for a double-thickness of felt and adding a little extra for covering the buttons.

**two** First measure the ready-made curtain along the length and width. For the border, you will need three strips of pink felt, each cut out in a double thickness. The length of two double-thickness strips should be the length of the curtain plus the depth of the border along the bottom and enough at the top to wrap round for a curtain rod loop, plus seam allowances of 2 cm ($^3/_4$ in) top and bottom. The length of the other double-thickness strip (which will go at the bottom of the curtain) should measure the width of the curtain plus the depth of the border on each side, plus seam allowances of 2 cm ($^3/_4$ in). The width of all three double-thickness strips should be twice the desired finished depth of the border, plus seam allowances of 2 cm ($^3/_4$ in). Here the strips have been cut to a width of 34 cm ($13^1/_2$ in) to create a finished 15 cm (6 in) deep border. Cut out the three strips and baste the double thicknesses together around the edges. They are now each treated at one strip.

**three** Press the border strips in half lengthwise, then open out. As if sewing bias binding, pin and stitch the two long strips to both sides of the curtain, right sides together, leaving the excess for the top curtain loop hanging at the top and the excess amount for the border hanging at the bottom. Repeat to attach the remaining strip to the bottom of the curtain, leaving the excess border fabric hanging evenly at both ends.

**four** To mitre each bottom corner, pull the two ends of the adjacent border strips to face each other and pin evenly together along the outside raw edges, right sides together. Stitch together from the end of the stitching in the corner to the outermost edge of the strip at an angle of 45°. Trim the excess and press open the diagonal seam.

**five** Fold the border over to the reverse side. The pressed line in the strips will be the folded edge of the border. Fold the corners to mitre them and make a sharp corner, pinning in place. Turn under a narrow hem along the long edge of each strip and pin so the edge of the velvet is hidden. Hand-stitch the corners to secure and machine- or hand-stitch with a hemming stitch along the long edges.

**six** At the top of the curtain, turn under the raw edges of the excess felt fabric and hand-stitch to create a neat finish.

**seven** Turn all the velvet tabs to the back of the curtain, along with the pink felt ends, and pin evenly in place. Make sure the curtain rod will easily slide through the loops you are making with the tabs and pink border. Stitch along the top width on the wrong side of the curtain to secure all the tabs in place.

**eight** Following the manufacturer's instructions, cover as many buttons as required in pink felt. Sew the buttons along the top of the curtain on top of each tab and one on each border end.

# Inglenook Cushions

Small cushions are an inventive way to use up old pieces of lace, pretty pearl buttons and offcuts. The frilled linen-coloured cushion in the background has a white embroidered front. The cushion to the left has been made from an ancient rectangular embroidered piece of linen, originally used as a small runner on top of a piece of furniture and now folded and stitched around a cushion pad, and the cushion to the right has been sewn from a length of pin-tucked fabric. In the foreground, a fine muslin square, decorated with tiny pearl buttons, has been caught by its corners onto the front face of a linen cushion.

The idea of an inglenook where one can cosily snuggle up next to a roaring fire with a good book is such an inviting treat. Although they look welcoming, these wooden seats can be hard, so make a squab seat cushion and some soft scatter cushions to add to your comfort. Here we chose light shades of cream and beige to contrast with the dark wood surround.

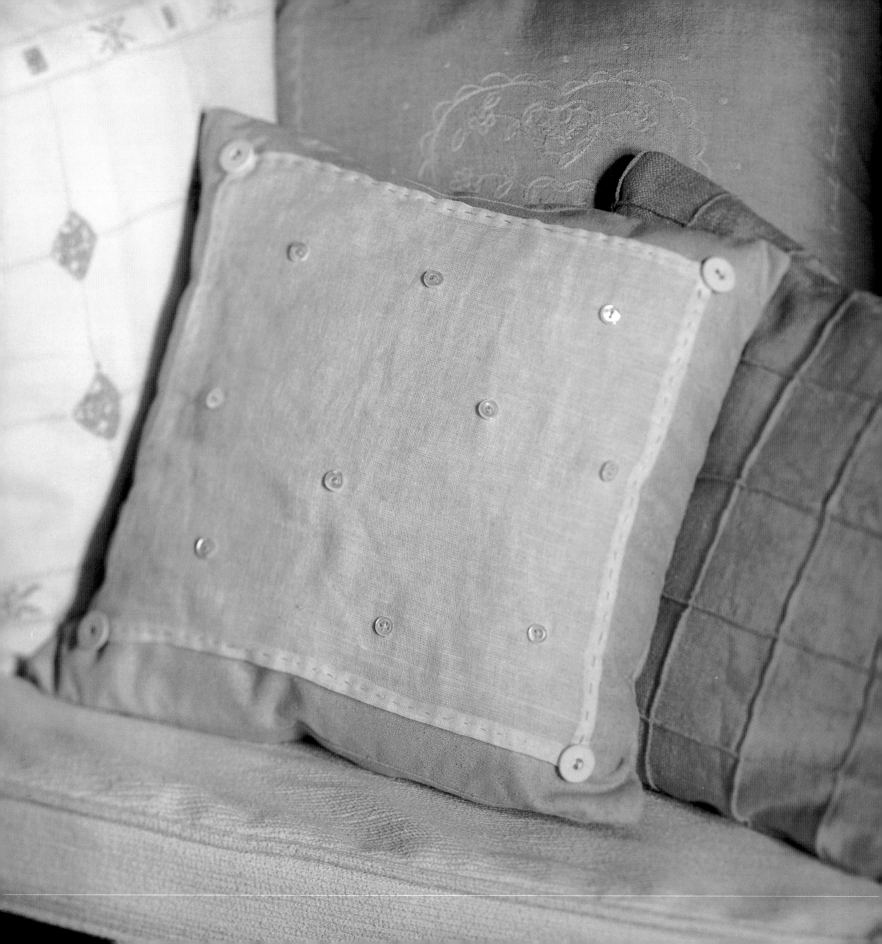

# Inglenook Squab

Piping is a very tidy way of finishing off a cushion for a window-seat or inglenook fireplace. Upholstery foam can be bought to the depth required, but make sure it conforms to current safety standards. To give a smoother effect, cover the foam with a layer of the thinnest wadding (batting) you can find. An off-white colour was chosen for this inglenook seat, but you can choose any colour of fabric that works with your interior decor. This seat is an irregular wedge-shape, and the instructions below will allow you to make a seat to any dimensions, whether rectangular, square or round. The opening for inserting and removing the foam cushion is placed at the back side of the seat.

MATERIALS

Paper and pencil

Foam, pre-cut to shape

Gridded pattern paper

Heavyweight linen or upholstery fabric, in amount to make the size of seat required (see step two)

Piping cord

Sewing thread to match the fabric

Zipper measuring about 5 cm (2 in) shorter than the length of the smaller 'gusset' strips (see step two)

**one** First make a paper template of the seat by measuring and marking the dimensions and shape of the seat on a piece of paper. Take the template to a foam supplier to cut the shape required.

**two** Measure and mark the pieces needed onto gridded pattern paper; seam allowances should be 1 cm ($\frac{1}{2}$ in). You will need two seat pieces which measure the size of the template plus seam allowances all round. You will need three 'gusset' or box strip pieces. The length of one piece should measure three-quarters the circumference of the seat, plus seam allowances on each end, and the width should be the depth of the upholstery foam plus seam allowances along each long side. The other two strip pieces will have a zipper fitted in them. The length of each one should measure one-quarter the circumference of the seat plus seam allowances on each end, and the width of each should measure half the depth of the foam plus seam allowances along each long side. To work out the amount of fabric needed, add up these totals. Add an extra 1 m (39 in) of fabric from which to cut bias binding for the piping.

**three** Cut out all the pieces from the fabric. Make 7.5 cm (3 in) wide bias binding by cutting the fabric on the diagonal and joining the lengths (see page 52). You need to have two lengths that each measure a little more than the circumference of the seat. Press the strips in half with wrong sides together, insert the piping cord and stitch to make the piping (see page 52).

**four** With the two narrow gusset strips right sides together, stitch from each end along one long side up to the zip positions. Press open the seam and insert a zipper in the seam on the wrong side. Join this short strip to the longer gusset strip at both short ends to make a continuous band.

**five** Pin and machine-stitch one length of the piping to the outside edge of the top seat piece on the right side. Repeat to pipe the bottom seat piece.

**six** With right sides together pin the gusset strip round the bottom seat piece, making sure the zipper is at the back position and the long raw edges are aligned. Using a zipper foot, machine-stitch as close as possible to the edge of the piping. Trim off the excess seam allowance, clip corners and press open the seam.

**seven** Open the zipper and repeat step 6 to attach the top seat piece to the gusset. Turn the seat cover right side out and insert the foam pad through the zipper opening.

bathrooms

# The bathroom

*must be the most neglected room in the house and yet it is the one room that everyone wants to escape to and relax in. Often bathrooms are needlessly cold and clinical, yet they can be made warm and inviting. Use sympathetic materials that are warm to the touch and available in natural colours, such as wooden Venetian blinds, tongue-and-groove boarding and wooden pegs. Consider shape, too. Rounded ceramic ware and roll-top cast-iron baths look and feel more inviting than hard angular shapes. In small and pokey bathrooms, create the feeling of light and space by replacing the doors with stained glass or sandblasted glass panels. Pale wall colours and generously sized mirrors will also increase the feeling of space.*

*Add luxury with soft fluffy towels, or towels dyed in your favourite colours. For a personal touch, towels, dressing gowns and slippers can all be monogrammed. Or you could make a laundry bag for each member of the family, such as a pretty beaded or sequinned one for a teenage daughter or a plain indigo-dyed one for a son. A stone bowl full of lovely soaps in intoxicating scents, such as lavender or lemon verbena, will make washing hands a special treat. Decant beautiful translucent bath oils into pretty bottles and arrange them on a shelf or surround the bath with tiny candles to make bathing a more romantic and relaxing experience.*

*A pile of beautiful soaps in glorious colours, made from natural ingredients and with rich creamy textures, are both luxurious and indulgent, guaranteeing the perfect bathtime.*

*Wet feet straight from the bath tub need a soft, absorbent surface to step onto. What could be simpler than to knit a bath mat from fabric remnants.*

### MATERIALS

White towels, as many
as required

Machine dyes in lilac,
blue, violet and sage
green, or colours of your
choice

Prewashed colourfast
cotton fabric remnants in
small-scale prints to
complement the towel
colours

Sewing threads in the
colours of the towels

# Trimmed Towels

Although towels can be bought in many colours, it is not always possible to find the exact shade you want. The towels here have been specially dyed and trimmed with small-print fabrics in pale colours. Use either authentic faded remnants or printed fabric reversed to the wrong side to create a more aged look. You could also use ribbons or pretty floral trims – there is usually a good selection to choose from in haberdashery (notions) shops.

**one**  Following the dye manufacturer's instructions, dye the towels in the washing machine. Use a separate wash for each colour. Tumble-dry the towels.

**two**  Cut two fabric strips for each towel (one for each end). Each strip should measure the length and width of the woven border of the towel, plus a 1.5 cm (⅝ in) hem allowance on all sides. If the towel has no woven border, cut the strip to measure the width of the towel, plus hem allowances on each end (the width of the strip can be any size desired).

**three**  On each fabric strip, press under 1.5 cm (⅝ in) along each side and each end. Pin the strip in place to cover the woven border, making sure it is straight and all raw edges are tucked under, and machine-stitch in place along all four sides.

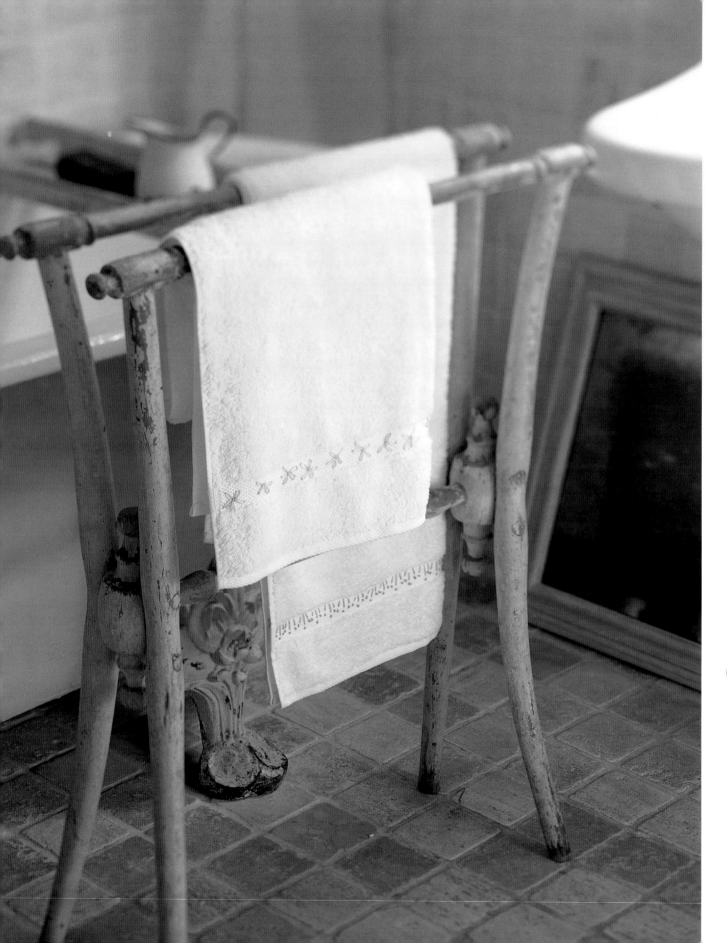

**MATERIALS**

White towels

Embroidery thread
(floss) (DMC green 563,
blue 747 and
yellow 726)

Embroidery needle

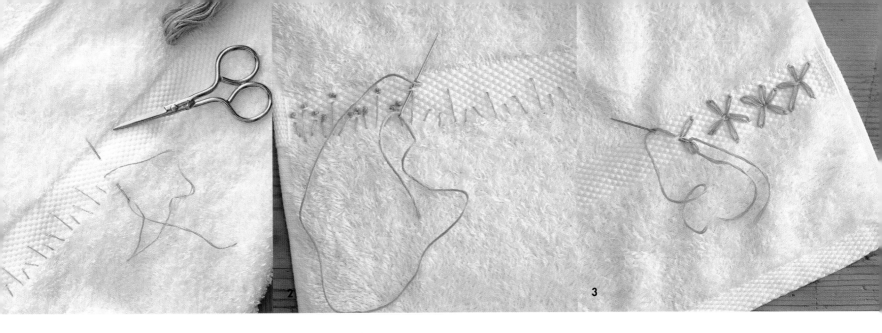

2

3

# Flower-embroidered Towels

What could be more luxurious than fluffy white towels? Perhaps pretty ones decorated with embroidered flowers. The inspiration for the designs given here is 1930s' cottage garden flowers. Six strands of embroidery thread (floss) were used for the designs so that the embroidery would stand out. Very simple stitches have been used here; for variety, chain stitch would also work well. Embroider matching sets of hand towels and bath sheets in colours to co-ordinate with your bathroom furnishings.

**one** For the field of flowers design, first stitch large straight stitches of different lengths in green embroidery thread (floss) along the border of the towel trim to act as the flower stems.

**two** Top each green flower stem with a French knot in blue embroidery thread (floss), made by tightly winding the embroidery thread twice around the needle before inserting the needle back into the towel at the original position.

**three** For the flower petal design, make long isolated daisy, or chain, stitches in blue embroidery thread. To do this, bring the needle up at a central position, create a loop with the thread to the desired size for the petal and re-insert the needle next to the original position. Then bring the needle up again at the outermost point, just inside the loop, and make a securing stitch to hold the loop in place. Return to a central position and repeat to make five flower petals. Make a row of flowers along the woven border of the towel. Finish with a yellow French knot (see step two) in the centre of each flower.

**MATERIALS**

Gridded pattern paper
and pencil

3.6 m (4 yd) of 115 cm
(45 in) wide pink-and-
white striped silk fabric

Tiny lavender, pink and
grey crystal beads and
a beading needle

Clothes hanger
(optional)

Extra silk fabric for
covering the clothes
hanger and for making
the heart sachet
(optional)

# Silk Kimono

Kimonos are elegant garments that look good on nearly everyone. Here the palest of pink-and-white striped silk is used, embellished with crystal beads sewn round the cuffs and front opening. For a more masculine version of this kimono, use heavyweight linen or waffle cotton. This pattern reaches to mid-calf, but can easily be extended to make an ankle-length robe.

**one**  Transfer the pattern supplied overleaf onto gridded pattern paper to the scale given. Copy each pattern piece square by square. Cut out the pattern pieces. Seam allowances are 1 cm ($^1/_2$ in) throughout.

**two**  Pin the pattern pieces onto the fabric. From the silk fabric, cut out one back, two fronts, two front placket pieces and a tie belt. Note that the back is cut from a double thickness of folded fabric – see the pattern piece overleaf for positioning. Lay the sleeve pattern as indicated by the arrow so the stripes run in the opposite direction to the body and cut out two pieces. Zigzag or finish all raw edges before assembling the kimono to prevent fraying. You will need to use the finest sewing-machine needle possible for stitching silk.

**three**  With right sides together, pin and stitch the body back to the body fronts at the shoulder seams. Open out and press seams open with the iron set to a low heat. With right sides together, pin and stitch one sleeve to the body at the armhole. Open out and press seams. Repeat to sew the other sleeve onto the body. Turn back, pin and machine-stitch a double hem at each sleeve cuff.

**four**  Re-fold the kimono in half with right sides together so the sleeves face outwards and the front pieces rest on the back piece. Align the raw edges and pin and machine-stitch along each side and inner arm to make a continuous seam that runs from the lower edge of the kimono to the hem of the cuff. Press seams open and turn right sides out. Turn under and press a double 2.5 cm (1 in) hem at the lower edge of the kimono; pin and secure with hemming stitch.

**five**  With right sides together, pin and stitch the two front placket pieces together, to create a long strip. Open out and press the seam flat. With right sides together, pin and stitch to the neck and front of robe. Press open and topstitch along the front seam for a neat finish.

**six**  Turn under the raw placket edge and press a double hem. Pin in place and secure to the wrong side of the front with hemming stitches.

**seven**  Make the belt by folding the fabric strip in half lengthwise with wrong sides together. Turn under, press and pin all raw edges to enclose them within the strip. Machine-stitch as close as possible to the turned-in edges.

**eight**  To finish, sew the beads at even intervals round the edge of the front opening and along the cuffs. If desired, cover a clothes hanger with matching silk fabric and sew a heart shape, fill it with lavender and decorate with beads, then hang from the clothes hanger.

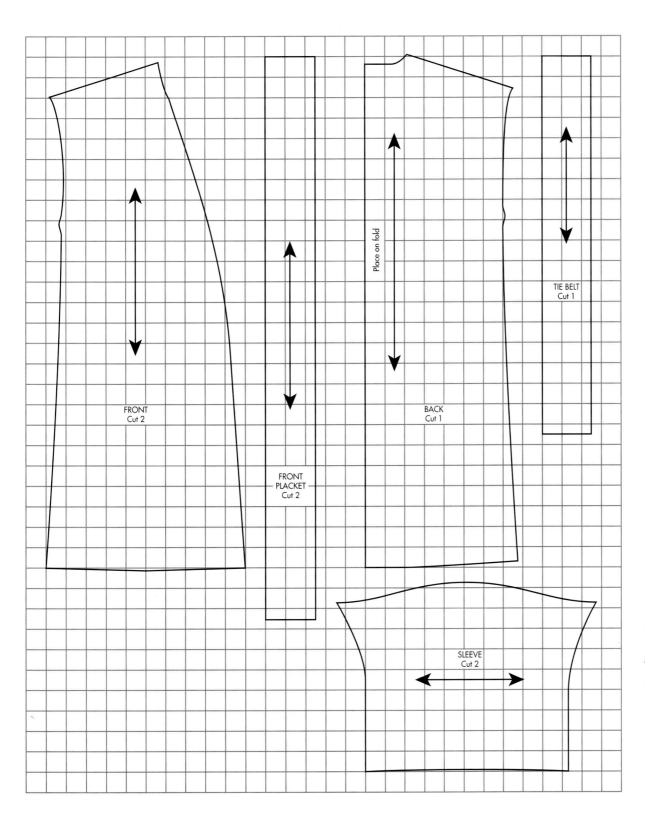

FRONT
Cut 2

FRONT
PLACKET
Cut 2

Place on fold

BACK
Cut 1

TIE BELT
Cut 1

SLEEVE
Cut 2

*The arrows on the pattern pieces*

*indicate the direction of the stripes.*

*Scale: one square on the pattern*

*pieces represents a 5 cm (2 in)*

*square on gridded pattern paper.*

### MATERIALS

2 pieces of linen, plain or printed, each
measuring 124 x 158 cm (49 x 62 in)

2 linen strips, plain or printed,
each measuring 4 cm x 1 m (1¹/₂ x 39 in)

Embroidery thread (floss)
(DMC white B5200) (optional)

Rocaille beads (optional)

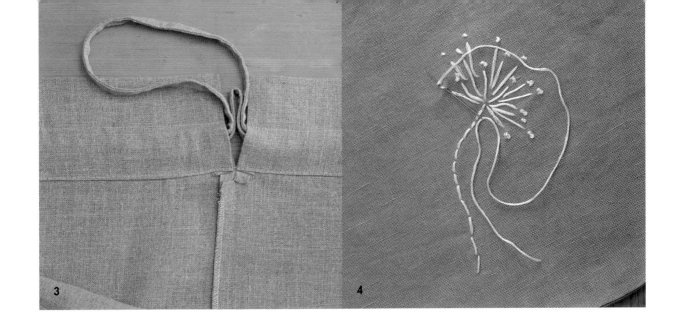

3

4

# Linen Laundry Bags

By making even the most mundane items appealing and beautiful, pleasure is added to life. Though simple laundry bags, these are made of the most beautiful linen. Here one has been embroidered, another beaded and the third left plain, as the weight of the linen and the deep colour needed no further enhancement. You may like to dye linen using a machine dye to achieve a deeply saturated colour, like the blue one pictured here.

**one**  With right sides together and using a 1 cm ($^1\!/_2$ in) seam allowance, pin and machine-stitch one piece of linen to the other along one short side. Pin and stitch along the two long sides, using a 1 cm ($^1\!/_2$ in) seam allowance and stopping 17 cm ($6^1\!/_2$ in) from the top on each side. Finish the raw edges and seams with a zigzag stitch. Press open the seam and the unstitched seam allowances at the sides.

**two**  With the seam allowances still turned in, fold over the top by 7.5 cm (3 in), turning under the raw edges of the open side. Machine-stitch around the top opening along the bottom edge of the fold, crossing the side seams. Sew another line of stitching 3 cm ($1^1\!/_4$ in) above the first line to create the casing or 'channel' for the ties. Turn the bag right side out and press.

**three**  Make the ties. Press the strips in half lengthwise with wrong sides together, then turn under and press all raw edges so they are hidden in the strip. Machine-stitch along the turned-in edges. Press flat. Thread the ties through the channel between the two lines of stitching by pinning one end to a large safety pin and pushing it through. Knot the ends of each length together.

**four**  Use a combination of straight stitches and French knots (see page 107) to embroider dandelion heads of different sizes all over the bag. Alternatively, if you are using a printed fabric, sew tiny rocaille beads onto the fabric to highlight parts of the printed pattern.

When one thinks of beadwork, it is usually in conjunction with something less utilitarian than a laundry bag. However, this floral fabric was just so pretty that it lent itself to further embellishment. The beads are simple rocailles in colours chosen to complement the shades of the fabric. They have been randomly stitched onto the flowers to highlight the pattern. You could also use beadwork to liven up plain linen bags, such as the ones shown on the previous page.

There is something very soothing and satisfying about beadwork, particularly when working on a random design such as this. Work in a good light and spread the beads out on a rimmed plate so you can see the various colours. After passing the needle through the bead, make a couple of small stitches in the fabric so that if the thread breaks, only one or two beads will fall off. The beaded areas grow quite quickly, so take care not to over-do the decoration. Keep the beading away from the drawstring top as the constant pulling could break the threads holding the beads in place.

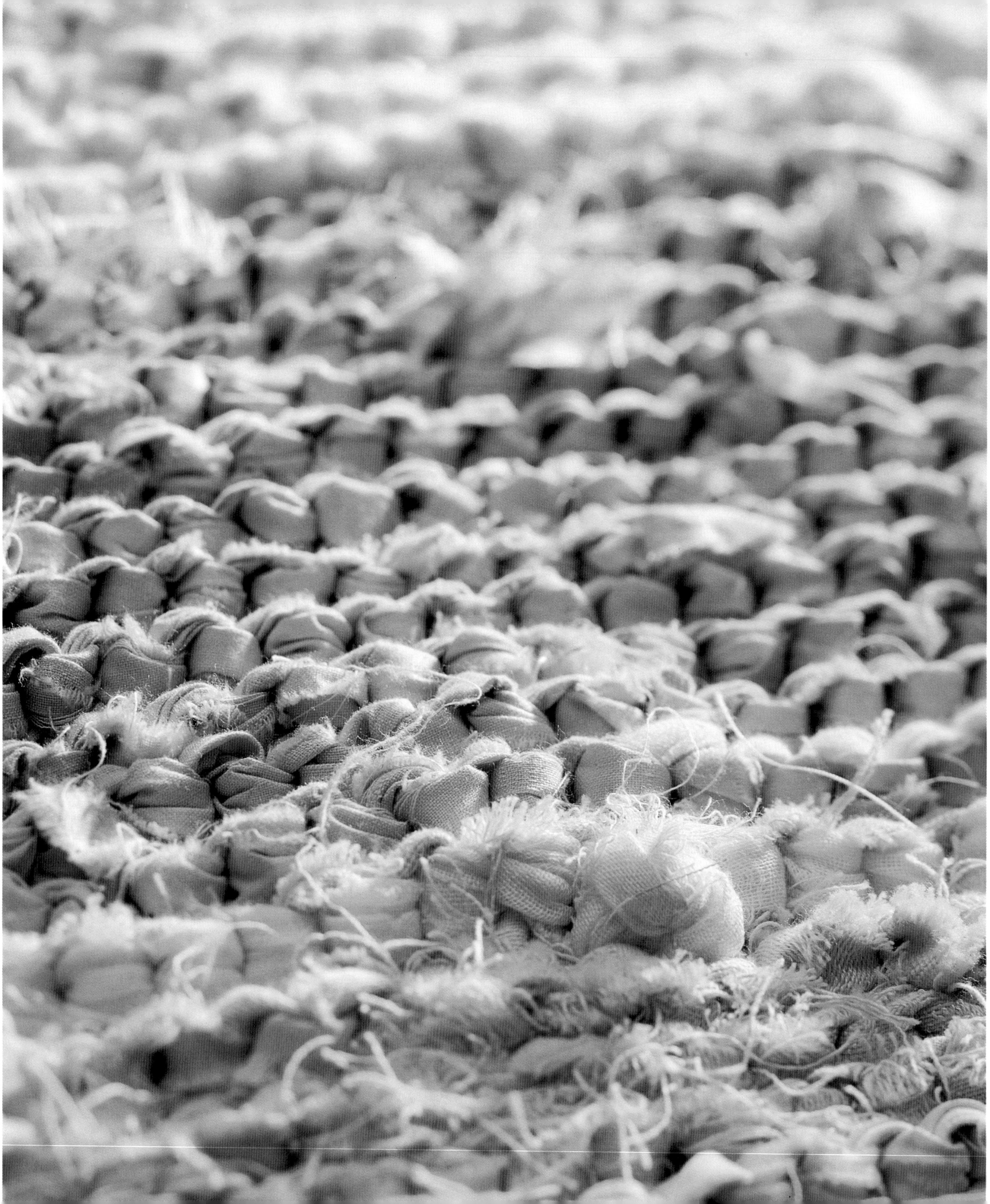

# Rag Rug Bathmat

This soft bath-side mat requires only the simplest of knitting skills and makes a cosy surface for wet feet. The amount of remnants needed to make this rug will depend on the thickness of the strips, their weight and the tension of the knitting. Here we have used cotton remnants in shades of cream and beige, plus some of the pink-and-white striped silk left over from the kimono featured earlier in this chapter. When worked with cotton strips, rag rug bathmats can be laundered in a washing machine.

**MATERIALS**

Remnants from natural fabrics, such as silk, cotton or linen, in a range of neutral shades

Size 7 or 8 knitting needles

**one** Prewash the remnants to ensure they are colourfast. Cut the fabric into 1 cm ($^1/_2$ in) wide strips. For wide pieces of fabric, cut the first strip to within 2 cm ($^3/_4$ in) of the end of the fabric and then turn at a right angle and carry on cutting round in a square to make a continuous long strip.

**two** Cast on 40 stitches and knit. Keep a loose tension, as it is difficult to slip tight thick stitches off big needles. Join different fabrics together by knotting them. When joining one strip to another, try to keep the tension the same. Join the fabrics with a flat reef knot to minimize the bumps.

**three** When the bathmat is the required size, cast off and push the knots through to the underside of the mat (the photo above left shows the front of the mat, the photo above right shows the back, with the knots and joins).

## Linen Guest Towels

These old-fashioned hand towels are inspired by 19th-century Hungarian cross-stitch and are beautiful examples of how effective simple borders can be on high-quality linen. The beauty of both the design and the fabric will make them well loved. Linen is an excellent fabric for hand towels as it is absorbent, is easy to wash and looks fresh and new after each laundering. The towels are made from heavy cream-coloured linen and the two short ends are finished with a drawn-thread technique.

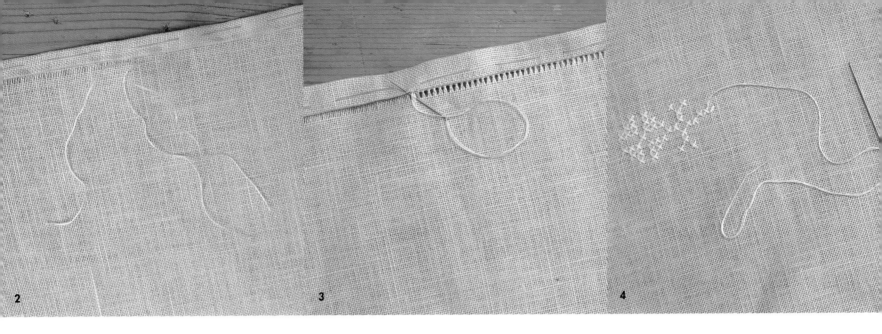

2  3  4

**MATERIALS**

Quality cream linen,
measuring 55 x 97 cm
(22 x 38 in)

Basting thread in a
dark colour

Hemming thread in the
same colour as the linen

2 skeins of embroidery
thread (floss)
(DMC white B5200)

Embroidery hoop or
frame (optional)

**one**  Make sure the linen piece is perfectly even, squaring up the edges as necessary. Turn under a narrow double hem along all the raw edges. Press flat and baste in place.

**two**  At each short end, gently pull out three weft (crosswise) threads just above the turned hem.

**three**  Using a hemming stitch, catch the warp (lengthwise) threads in threes as you stitch the hem. As you do this, a pretty triangular pattern will be created along the hem. Hem the long sides of the towel hem by folding, pinning and pressing a double hem, then stitching in place. Measure 10–12 cm (4–4³/₄ in) up from each short end and baste a row of stitches parallel to each end, keeping the line very straight and even.

**four**  Cross-stitch along the basted line, following one of the border pattern charts on the right and using two strands of embroidery thread (floss) (see also page 29). Work at about four stitches per centimetre (ten stitches per inch). If desired, stretch the linen taut in an embroidery hoop or frame while working the cross-stitch. When the border is completed, remove the basting stitches and press the hand towel flat.

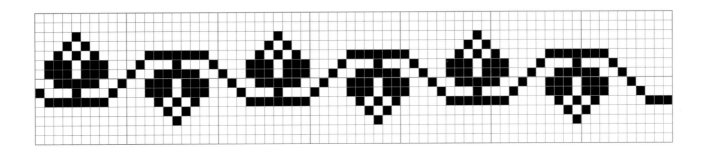

**MATERIALS**

Sheet of plastic, from a thick plastic bag or
a clean food container

Spirit-based marker pen and scissors

225 g (8 oz) carded slivers of merino wool fleece,
in mauve, pale blue and pale salmon colours

75 g (3 oz) masham wool in a neutral colour

Soap flakes

Spray bottle or mister

Split-cane blind or beach mat

Rolling pin

# Felt Slippers

Felt – simply fleece that has been treated with soap and water and then shrunk and beaten into shape – was one of the earliest ways of making cloth. It is still used for clothing today, especially in cold countries. Here a warm, colourful pair of slippers is just the thing for winter evenings. The rolling and soaking process employed in felting the wool also mixes different colours of wool together, creating a muted multicoloured effect.

**one** For each slipper make a plastic template that is about one-third larger than the desired size of the slipper. To do this, draw round your foot and then enlarge the shape on a photocopier. Simplify the shape so it is very rounded. Use a spirit-based pen and scissors to mark and cut the two shapes out of the plastic.

**two** For each slipper, lay the fleece so that all the fibres run in the same direction over the template. The fibres should generously overlap the template.

**three** Dissolve two handfuls of soap flakes in a jug of hot water, using slightly more than if washing a jumper. Fill a spray bottle or plant mister with some of the solution. Spray the fibres with the soapy water to wet it well. Make a second layer with the fibres running in the opposite direction. Spray again with the soapy water. Turn the template over and repeat the two-layer process. Finish the underside of each slipper with a layer of the coarser masham wool.

**four** Carefully cut out an oval in the top layer as the opening for the foot.

**five** Place a wet soapy slipper in the cane blind or mat. Roll the blind up and roll it backward and forward until the wool becomes matted and felted. The slipper will look enormous at this stage, but don't worry. Repeat with the other slipper.

**six** Lay the slippers flat and allow to dry. When they have hardened, remove the template. Machine-wash the slippers in a 40°C (104°F) wash. Tumble-dry the slippers on a low heat for 5–10 minutes to help create the round shape.

**seven** While still damp, mould and beat the slippers into shape using a rolling pin pushed into the ends. At this stage, also adjust the size of the opening slit to fit the foot. Keep moulding the slippers periodically until they are completely dry.

# Hooded Bath Towel

Make your own baby bath towel from the softest towelling (terrycloth). The hood, which is attached diagonally over one corner of the towelling square, makes it easier to keep the towel wrapped around a wet and wriggling baby. Mix tiny-scale gingham with a flower-print cotton for a pretty piped edge and use two layers of towelling to make it extra cosy and ultra-absorbent. If making the towel as a present for a newborn baby, you could embroider the child's name or initials on the hood or across one corner (see page 47 for a cross-stitch alphabet chart).

**MATERIALS**

1.2 m (1¹/₃ yd) of
170 cm (68 in) wide
white towelling
(terrycloth)

White sewing thread

1 m (39 in) pink
gingham fabric

1 m (39 in) flower-print
cotton fabric

4 m (4¹/₃ yd) of the
narrowest piping cord
you can find

**one**  Prewash the towelling (terrycloth), gingham and flower-print fabric to ensure they are preshrunk and colourfast. Cut two pieces of towelling each measuring 82 cm x 1 m (32 x  39 in). Lay the pieces on top of each other and cut the corners to round them. Pin and machine-stitch around the circumference through both thicknesses, using a 1 cm (¹/₂ in) seam allowance.

**two**  Cut two right triangles from the white towelling, each measuring 20 cm (8 in) from the centre of the long side to the opposite corner and 30 cm (12 in) from this corner to each outside point. Round this corner so it will fit over one corner of the towel. Stitch the two triangles on top of each other, as in step one.

**three**  Pin and machine-stitch the triangle to one corner of the towel to form the hood.

**four**  Make the bias binding. Fold the gingham fabric diagonally so that one raw edge is even with the selvedge. Press the fold; it is the bias line. Unfold the fabric. Measure and mark 3 cm (1¹/₄ in) wide parallel lines along the bias. Cut the strips. Place the ends of two strips at right angles to each other, with right sides together. Position the strips so that when joined with a 5 mm (¹/₄ in) seam on the straight grain, the raw edges of the resulting bias strip will be even. Stitch the seam and press open, trimming off the points of the seam allowance at right angles to each other. Continue to join ends as necessary to create two lengths, one to bind the hood opening edge and one to bind round the entire towel. Repeat for the flower fabric, but cut the strips 4 cm (1¹/₂ in) wide.

**five**  Fold each gingham strip in half lengthwise with wrong sides together and press. Turn under the raw edges at the short ends of each strip for a neat finish. Place a length of piping cord inside each strip along the fold and pin at the top to hold it in place. Using the zipper foot on the sewing machine, stitch along the length of each strip, as close to the cord as possible and keeping raw edges even.

**six**  With the raw edge facing outwards and aligning with the edge of the towelling, pin the shorter length of piping to the top side of the hood at the front. Machine-stitch 1 cm (¹/₂ in) from the edge.

**seven**  Pin the flower binding right side down along the edge of the hood opening and on top of the piping. Make sure the ends have been turned under to create a neat finish. Using the zipper foot, stitch along the edge as close as possible to the piping.

**eight**  Press open and fold the flower binding to the underside of the towelling, enclosing all the raw edges. Turn under and press the raw edge. Pin in place on the underside of the towelling and secure with a hemming stitch.

**nine**  Repeat steps six–eight to stitch the gingham piping and flower binding round the circumference of the towel. Overlap the binding to join the ends neatly.

# Contributors

*The author and publisher would like to thank the following companies for props and supplies:*

**Andrew Martin International**
(suede on the roll)
200 Walton Street
London SW3 2JL
Telephone 020 7225 5100

**B. Brown**
(display materials and felt)
Customer Service Centre
74–78 Wood Lane End
Hemel Hempstead
Hertfordshire HP2 4RF
Telephone 0870 534 0340

**Couverture**
(slippers on page 7; bedcovers and cushions)
310 Kings Road
London SW3 5UH
Telephone 020 7795 1200

**Creative Beadcraft Ltd**
(beads, feathers and trimmings by mail order)
Denmark Works
Sheepcote Dell Road
Beamond End
Near Amersham
Buckinghamshire HP7 ORX
Telephone 01494 715606

**Damask**
3-4 Broxholme House
New Kings Road
London SW6 4AA
Telephone 020 7731 3553

**DMC**
(embroidery threads, waste canvas and linen)
Creative World
Pullman Road
Wigston
Leicester LE8 2DY
Telephone 0116 281 1040

**Dylon International Ltd**
(for all the dyes used throughout the book)
Worsley Bridge Road
London SE26 5HD
Telephone 020 8663 4296

**Highly Sprung Ltd**
(for the loan of sofas and Liz Hankey who organized it)
185-186 Tottenham Court Road
London W1P 9LE
Telephone 020 7631 1424

**Ian Mankin**
(fabric)
271 Wandsworth Bridge Road
London SW6 2TX
Telephone 020 7371 8825

**Josephine Ryan Antiques and Interiors**
63 Abbeville Road
London SW4 9JW
Telephone 020 8675 3900

**Laura Ashley**
(fabric for Baby Sleeping Bag and the floral Linen Laundry Bag)
Telephone 0870 562 2116 for stockists

**Lilliput**
(Donald Mackenzie cot)
255 Queenstown Road
London SW8 3NP
Telephone 020 7720 5554

**McCullock and Wallis**
(silk dupion and linen)
25 Dering Street
London W1S 1AT
Telephone 020 7629 0311

**Molton Brown**
(cosmetics, soaps and oils)
58 South Molton Street
London W1Y 1HH
Telephone 020 7518 1430

**Natural Fabric Company**
(hessian curtain material)
Wessex Place
127 High Street
Hungerford
Berkshire RG17 0DL
Telephone 01488 684002

**Ocean**
(felt rug and suede cushions)
689 Mitcham Road
Croydon
Surrey CRO 3AF
Telephone 0870 242 6283

**Price's Candles**
110 York Road
London SW11 3RU
Telephone 020 7801 2030

**Shaker**
(sheets and oval coffee table box)
72–73 Marylebone High Street
London W1M 3AR
Telephone 020 7935 9461

**Wild Jewellery Company**
(stone buttons)
7 Grove Park Terrace
London W4 3JL
Telephone 020 8994 6322

**Wimbledon Sewing Machine Company**
(fabrics)
296 and 312 Balham High Road
London SW17 7AA
Telephone 020 8767 0036